장화홍련전

The Story of Janghwa and Hongryeon

머리말

"다락원 한국어 학습 문고" 시리즈는 대표적인 한국 문학 작품을 한국어 학습자들의 읽기 수준에 맞도록 재구성하여 쉽고 재미있게 독해력을 증진할 수 있도록 하였습니다. '국제 통용 한국어 표준 교육 과정'과 '한국어 교육 어휘 내용 개발'을 기준으로 초급부터 고급(A1~C2)으로 구분하여 지문을 읽으면서 각자의 수준에 맞는 필수 어휘와 표현을 자연스럽게 익힐 수 있습니다.

시대적 배경과 관련된 어휘에는 별도의 설명을 추가하여 그 당시 문화에 대해 이해하면서 본문을 읽을 수 있도록 하였습니다. 더불어 의미 전달에 충실한 번역문과 내용 이해 문제를 수록하여 자신의 이해 정도를 점검하고 확인할 수 있도록 하였고, 전문 성우가 직접 낭독한 음원을 통해 눈과 귀를 동시에 활용한 독해 연습이 가능하도록 하였습니다.

"다락원 한국어 학습 문고" 시리즈를 통해 보다 유익하고 재미있는 한국어 학습이 되시길 바랍니다.

다락원 한국어 학습 문고
편저자 대표 **김유미**

Preface

The Darakwon Korean Readers series adapts the most well-known Korean literary works to the reading levels of Korean language learners, restructuring them into simple and fun stories that encourage the improvement of reading comprehension skills. Based on the "International Standard Curriculum for the Korean Language" and "Research on Korean Language Education Vocabulary Content Development", the texts have been graded from beginner to advanced levels (A1~C2) so that readers can naturally learn the necessary vocabulary and expressions that match their level.

With supplementary explanations concerning historical background, learners can understand the culture of the era as they read. In addition, students can assess and confirm their understanding with the included reading comprehension questions and translations faithful to the meaning of the original text. Recordings of the stories by professional voice actors also allow reading practice through the simultaneous use of learners' eyes and ears.

We hope that Darakwon Korean Readers series will provide learners with a more fruitful and interesting Korean language learning experience.

Darakwon Korean Readers
Kim Yu Mi, Lead Adapter

일러두기

How to Use This Book

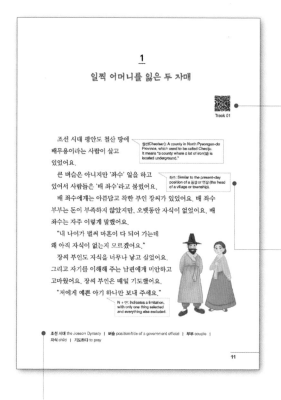

듣기 Listening

QR 코드를 통해 전문 성우가 녹음한 정확하고 생생한 작품 낭독을 들을 수 있습니다.

Using the corresponding QR codes, learners can access professional recordings of the story.

해설 Notes

학습자들이 내용을 이해하는 데 필요한 한국어 문법, 표현, 어휘, 속담, 문화적 배경 등을 알기 쉽게 설명해 주어 별도로 사전을 찾을 필요가 없도록 하였습니다.

Explanations on essential Korean grammar, expressions, vocabulary, proverbs, cultural background, etc. are provided to learners so aid understanding without the need to consult a separate dictionary.

어휘 설명 Vocabulary Explanation

각 권의 수준에 맞춰 본문에서 꼭 알아야 하는 필수 어휘를 영어 번역과 함께 제시하였습니다.

English translations are provided for the essential vocabulary matched to the level of each title.

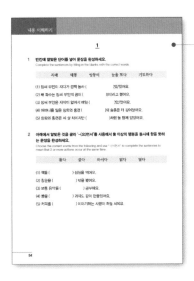

내용 이해하기 Reading Comprehension

다양한 문제를 통해 본문 내용 이해와 함께 해당 레벨에서 알아야 할 문형과 어휘를 다시 한번 확인할 수 있습니다.

Learners can check their understanding of the main text while also reviewing the essential sentence patterns and vocabulary for their level through various comprehension questions.

본문 번역 Text Translations

한국어 본문 내용을 정확히 이해할 수 있도록 의미 전달에 충실한 영어 번역을 수록하였습니다.

An English translation faithful to the original text is included to ensure an exact understanding of the original Korean story.

모범 답안 Answers

모범 답안과 비교하며 자신의 이해 정도를 스스로 평가하고 진단할 수 있습니다.

Learners can self-evaluate and assess their level of understanding by comparing their answers to the answer key.

작품 소개

장화홍련전

　사또가 새로 부임해 왔다 하면 그날 밤 바로 죽어 나가는 마을이 있었어요. 많은 사람들이 사또를 지키고 있어도 소용이 없었어요. 그러던 어느 날, 현명하고 용감한 한 사또가 그 마을로 가게 되었어요. 이 사또는 어떻게 되었을까요? '장화홍련전'의 이야기는 이렇게 시작됩니다.

　"장화홍련전"은 조선 시대의 실제 사건을 바탕으로 쓰인 소설입니다. 착하고 예쁜 두 딸, 장화와 홍련은 어린 나이에 억울하게 죽은 뒤 귀신이 되었어요. 자신들의 이야기를 들어주는 사람을 찾아 밤마다 사또들의 방을 찾아갔지만, 사또들은 귀신이 자신을 해칠 것이라고 생각하여 겁을 먹은 나머지 놀라 죽어 버렸어요. 겉모습만 보고 판단했기 때문이에요. 마찬가지로 사람들도 사또들이 죽은 이유를 모두 귀신 때문이라고 생각했어요.

　만약 여러분들이 자신이 한 일이 아닌데도 억울하게 의심받게 되면 마음이 어떨까요? 그리고 그 이야기를 아무도 들어주지 않는다면 그 마음은 또 어떨까요? 아마 무척이나 답답하고 속상할 것입니다. 나쁜 사람들의 거짓말에 속아 죽임을 당한 장화와 홍련의 입장을 떠올리며 이야기를 읽어 봅시다. 한편, 두 자매의 억울함을 현명하고 용감한 사또가 어떻게 풀어 주었는지 읽다 보면, 조금은 통쾌한 마음이 들지도 모릅니다. 장화와 홍련의 이야기를 읽으면서 옛날 사람들의 마음을 느껴 봅시다.

Introduction to the Story

The story of Janghwa and Hongryeon

There was once a village where every new magistrate died the very same night they took up their post there. Even if many people watched over the magistrate, it was no use. But then one day, a wise and brave magistrate was dispatched to the village. What became of that magistrate? This is how "The Story of Janghwa and Hongryeon" begins.

"The Story of Janghwa and Hongryeon" is a novel that was written based on a real incident in the Joseon Dynasty. After dying unfairly at a young age, two kind and beautiful daughters, Janghwa and Hongryeon, became ghosts. Looking for someone who would listen to their story, they visited the rooms of the magistrates each night, but the magistrates thought the ghosts would hurt them, and, terrified, all died of fright. This is because they made judgements based only on appearances. Similarly, all of the people thought that the magistrates had died because of the ghosts.

If you were unfairly suspected of something you hadn't done, how would you feel? And if nobody would listen to your story? How would you feel then? It would probably be very frustrating and upsetting. Try reading this story while imagining the perspective of Janghwa and Hongryeon, who met their deaths after being deceived by the lies of wicked people. On the other hand, when you read about how the wise and brave magistrate resolved the injustice faced by the two sisters, you might feel a little bit better. Try to feel the emotions of these people in the past as you read Janghwa and Hongryeon's story.

목차

Table of Contents

장화홍련전

The Story of Janghwa and Hongryeon

등장인물
characters

장화
Janghwa

홍련의 언니예요. 예쁘고 착해요. 새어머니의 속임수 때문에 연못에 빠져 죽어요.

Hongryeon's older sister. She is beautiful and kind. Due to her stepmother's tricks, she falls into the pond and dies.

홍련
Hongryeon

장화의 여동생이에요. 언니를 닮아 예쁘고 착해요. 언니가 죽었다는 것을 알고 따라 죽어요.

Janghwa's younger sister. Beautiful and kind, like her older sister. When she learns her sister has died, she follows her and dies too.

배 좌수
Bae Jwasu

장화, 홍련의 아버지예요. 장화와 홍련의 어머니가 세상을 떠나자 허씨를 아내로 맞이해요.

Janghwa and Hongryeon's father. After Janghwa and Hongryeon's mother passes away, he takes Lady Heo as his wife.

허씨 부인
Lady Heo

장화, 홍련의 새어머니예요. 장화와 홍련을 몹시 괴롭혀요. 장화가 시집갈 때 가져갈 재산이 아까워 장화를 해치려고 해요.

Janghwa and Hongryeon's stepmother. She torments Janghwa and Hongryeon terribly. When it comes time for Janghwa to marry, she is greedy for the inheritance the girl will take and decides to hurt Janghwa.

장쇠
Jangswe

허씨 부인의 첫째 아들이에요. 허씨 부인의 말만 들어요. 착한 장화를 해치게 되고 나중에 벌을 받아요.

Lady Heo's first son. He only listens to lady Heo. He hurts the kind Janghwa and gets punished later.

정동우
Jeong Dongwu

철산 사또예요. 용기 있고 똑똑해요. 귀신이 되어 나타난 장화와 홍련의 사연을 듣고 두 자매를 도와줘요.

The magistrate of Cheolsan. Brave and clever. He listens to the story of Janghwa and Hongryeon who appear to him as ghosts and helps the two sisters.

1
일찍 어머니를 잃은 두 자매

Track 01

　조선 시대 평안도 철산 땅에
배무용이라는 사람이 살고
있었어요.

> 철산(Cheolsan): A county in North Pyeongan-do Province, which used to be called Cheolju. It means "a county where a lot of iron(철) is located underground."

　큰 벼슬은 아니지만 '좌수' 일을 하고
있어서 사람들은 '배 좌수'라고 불렀어요.

> 좌수: Similar to the present-day position of a 동장 or 면장 (the head of a village or township).

　배 좌수에게는 아름답고 착한 부인 장씨가 있었어요. 배 좌수
부부는 돈이 부족하지 않았지만, 오랫동안 자식이 없었어요. 배
좌수는 자주 이렇게 말했어요.

　"내 나이가 벌써 마흔이 다 되어 가는데
왜 아직 자식이 없는지 모르겠어요."

　장씨 부인도 자식을 너무나 낳고 싶었어요.
그리고 자기를 이해해 주는 남편에게 미안하고
고마웠어요. 장씨 부인은 매일 기도했어요.

　"저에게 예쁜 아기 하나만 보내 주세요."

> N + 만: Indicates a limitation, with only one thing selected and everything else excluded.

조선 시대 the Joseon Dynasty　|　벼슬 position/title of a government official　|　부부 couple　|
자식 child　|　기도하다 to pray

그러던 어느 날 장씨 부인이 피곤해서 잠깐 잠이 들었어요.
꿈속에서 한 선녀가 하늘에서 내려와 꽃을 한 송이 주었어요. 장씨
부인은 꽃을 받아 가슴에 안았어요. 그런데 그 꽃이 아름다운 선녀로
변해 장씨 부인의 가슴 속으로 들어왔어요. 장씨 부인이 깜짝 놀라
눈을 떴어요.

장씨 부인은 배 좌수에게 꿈 이야기를 했어요.

"어젯밤에 아주 이상한 꿈을 꾸었어요."

"무슨 꿈을 꾸었습니까?"

장씨 부인의 이야기를 듣고 배 좌수는 매우 기뻐하며 말했어요.

"부인, 그건 태몽입니다. 우리 부부가 자식이 없는 것을 하늘이
알고 자식을 보내 주려는 것 같아요."

> 태몽: A dream that informs you that you're pregnant (conception dream).

"정말일까요? 그렇게만 된다면 정말 좋겠어요."

그리고 열 달이 되자 장씨

> V/A + -면: A connective ending indicating that the following word serves as the reason or condition for the preceding word.

부인은 정말 너무도 예쁜 아이를
낳았어요. 아기의 이름은 '장화'였어요. 꽃처럼 아름다운 딸이라는
뜻이에요. 부부는 아이가 태어나서 너무나
행복했고 아이를 너무나 사랑했어요.

> N + 처럼: Indicates that something is the target of a metaphor or comparison, and expresses that this and a state or action are similar or the same.

장화가 세 살이 되었을 때 배 좌수 부부에게
두 번째 아이가 찾아왔어요. 배 좌수 부부는 이번에는 남자아이가
태어나기를 바랐어요.

> · V/A + -(으)ㄹ 때: Indicates a moment in time at which an action or situation occurs, or the period during which it continues.
> · 바라다: When using the form "V + -기를 바라다," "바라-" + "았" becomes "바랐-" and not "바랬-."

선녀 fairy/angel (in Taoism) | **송이** counter word for flowers or clusters of fruit | **가슴** chest, breast | **변하다** to change | **눈을 뜨다** (lit. to open one's eyes) to wake up | **이상하다** to be strange

그러나 이번에도 여자아이였어요. 배 좌수 부부는 조금 섭섭했지만 태어난 아기를 보고 기뻐했어요. 둘째 딸의 이름을 붉은 연꽃을 뜻하는 '홍련'으로 지었어요.

> N + (으)로: A particle that indicates qualification or status, followed by the verb "짓다" when used with a name noun.

장화와 홍련은 잘 자랐어요. 세 살 차이지만 쌍둥이처럼 꼭 붙어 다녔어요. 같이 이야기도 하고 춤도 추고 소꿉놀이도 하면서 친하게 지냈어요.

> · 소꿉놀이: Refers to the children's game of playing with toys like bowls and plates, called "소꿉."
> · V/A + -(으)면서: Indicates that two or more actions or states are occurring at the same time.

그러나 좋은 일 뒤에는 항상 나쁜 일이 따라오는 것 같아요. 장씨 부인이 그만 병에 걸려 자리에 눕고 말았어요. 장화의 나이 일곱 살, 홍련의 나이 네 살 때였어요. 일곱 살인 장화는 아버지 배 좌수와 함께 장씨의 옆을 떠나지 않고 장씨가 약 먹는 것을 매일 같이 도왔어요. 좋다는 약은 다 써 봤지만 장씨의 병은 낫지 않았어요.

"부인, 어린 딸들을 생각해서 제발 일어나세요."

"미안해요, 여보. 불쌍한 우리 애들 두고 어떻게 눈을 감을 수 있을지……."

> 눈을 감다 (lit. to close one's eyes): For a person's life to end, or in other words, "to die."

섭섭하다 to be disappointed | 붉다 to be red | 연꽃 lotus flower | 차이 (age) difference | 쌍둥이 twins | 붙어 다니다 to go around together | 따라오다 to follow | 자리에 눕다 to be bedridden (with an illness) | 병이 낫다 to recover from a disease | 제발 please | 불쌍하다 to be pitiable, to be poor

"어머니, 그런 말씀 하지 마세요. 얼른 이 약 드시고 건강히 일어나세요. 네?"

그러나 장씨 부인의 몸이 점점 약해지고 살도 점점 빠졌어요. 숨도 잘 못 쉬었어요. 장씨 부인은 겨우 숨을 쉬며 배 좌수에게 말했어요.

"여보, 제가 죽으면…… 우리 두 딸, 장화와 홍련이를 잘 부탁합니다. 저 불쌍한…… 아이들을 잘 키워서, 좋은 사람과 결혼해 오래오래 행복하게 살게 해…… 주세요. 제…… 소원을 들어주시면, 죽어서도…… 고마움을 잊지 않겠어요."

"왜 그런 말을 하는 거예요? 걱정하지 말고 얼른 일어나세요."

"제가 죽고 나면…… 새 아내가 들어와 아이들이 아버지의 사랑을 못 받을까 봐 걱정돼요.

야, 약속, 해, 주…… 주세요.

장화, 홍……련이, 잘 부탁…….."

> V/A + -(으)ㄹ까 보다: Indicates speculation worrying about an action or situation. Used when one's speculation is worrying or concerning.

장씨 부인이 힘들게 손을 들자 배 좌수가 그 손을 잡고 말했어요.

"약속할게요. 그런 걱정은 하지 말고 일어나세요."

있는 힘을 다해 말을 마친 장씨 부인은 눈을 감았어요.

"부인! 부인!"

"어머니! 어머니!"

드시다 to eat (polite) | 약하다 to be weak | 빠지다 to lose (strength, weight, etc.) | 겨우 barely |
소원 wish | 잊다 to forget | 다하다 to exhaust

배 좌수가 울기 시작했고 장화도 어린 홍련을 안고 엉엉 울었어요.

장씨 부인을 산에 모시고
장화와 홍련은 너무 슬퍼서
잠도 자지 않고 울기만 했어요.
시간이 흘러 장씨의 삼년상을 마쳤지만, 어머니를 잃은
장화, 홍련 자매의 슬픔은
더욱 깊어 갔어요.

> N에 모시다 (lit. to bring N somewhere): If used with the nouns 산 (mountain) and 묘지 (burial place), it means to bury a person's body in a certain place.

> **TIP!** 삼년상: Refers to being in mourning for a period of 3 years when one's parent passes away. "상" refers to refraining from activities and abstaining from behaviors for a set period of time in order to commemorate a relative when they have passed away.

안다 to hold | 엉엉 sound or manner of crying loudly and unrestrainedly | 마치다 to finish, to end |
자매 sisters | 깊다 to be deep

2

성격 나쁜 새어머니, 허씨 부인

Track 02

장씨 부인이 떠난 지
삼 년이 지났어요. 더 이상

> V + -(으)ㄴ 지: Used when indicating how long it has been since something was done.

집안에서 웃음소리와 노랫소리가 나오지 않았어요. 장화와 홍련은
말없이 외롭게 자랐어요. 슬퍼하는 딸들의
모습을 지켜보는 아버지의 마음도 너무

> 마음에 걸리다 (lit. to be hung in one's mind): For one's mind to be unsatisfied and uncomfortable.

아팠어요. 배 좌수는 죽은 아내의 말이 마음에 걸렸지만 대를 이을
아들이 없어서 걱정이 많았어요.

> TIP! 대를 잇다 (lit. to continue generations): The act of not breaking a bloodline and family tree that has been passed down in a family. In the past, it was thought that sons, especially eldest sons, carried on a family's name.

또 딸들이 엄마 없이 지내는
모습을 더 이상 보고 싶지
않아서 다시 결혼하기로 했어요.

> V + -기로 하다: Indicates having planned or decided something. Used when making a suggestion or promise to the listener, or when talking about your own determinations or decisions.

외롭다 to be lonely | **자라다** to be raised | **결혼하다** to marry

배 좌수는 이 사람 저 사람에게 부탁하여 장화와 홍련의 새엄마 될 사람을 찾았어요.

"우리 딸아이들을 잘 키워 주고 우리 집안 대를 이어 줄 튼튼한 사람이면 좋겠어요."

여기저기 사람을 소개받았지만 하나같이 약해 보여서 마음에 들지 않았어요. 그중에 허씨 성을 가진 여자가 가장 튼튼해 보였어요.

허씨를 처음 본 배 좌수는 깜짝 놀랐어요. 얼굴에는 무언가 잔뜩 났고 두 눈은 너무 컸고, 입은 앞으로 나와 있고, 허리는 굵고 다리는 코끼리 다리 같았어요. 오래 쳐다보기 어려울 정도로 못생긴 모습이었고 성격은 더욱 나빴어요.

그렇지만 몸만 튼튼하면 괜찮다고 생각해서 배 좌수는 허씨와 결혼했어요. 그런데 이런! 허씨가 시집온 첫날부터 어린 장화와 홍련을 좋게 보지 않아서 집안 분위기가 많이 바뀌었어요. 날마다 집안이 시끄러웠고 큰 소리가 계속 났어요.

> · N + 마다: A particle that means "each and every one" of something without missing any.
> · V/A: + -(이)냐: Sentence-closing ending indicating a question. Mainly used a lot in conversational language.

"그건 또 무엇이냐? 왜 남은 음식을 남의 집에 주는 것이냐? 다시 가져와라."

"어서 가서 풀을 잘라서 거름을 더 많이 만들어 놓아라!"

"어서 일어나 일을 하고 나무도 해 와라."

> V + -아라/어라/해라: Used when the speaker orders the listener to perform an action.

새엄마 stepmother | 키우다 to raise | 튼튼하다 to be strong, to be healthy | 보이다 to look, to seem | 성 surname | 가장 most | 잔뜩 extremely | 코끼리 elephant | 쳐다보다 to stare | 못생기다 to be ugly | 시집오다 for a woman to get married (lit. to come to one's husband's house [시집] after marriage) | 바뀌다 to change | 시끄럽다 to be noisy | 거름 manure

허씨는 하인들에게 계속 일을 시켰어요. 또한 장화와 홍련도 그냥 두지 않았어요. 딸들에게 쉬지 않고 일을 시켰어요.

"너희들은 이 옷을 내일까지 다시 만들어 놓아라!"

"또 방 안에서 놀고 있는 것이냐? 할 일이 없으면 이 고추를 하나씩 햇빛이 들어오는 곳에 잘 두어라."

하인 servant | 또한 additionally, as well | 그냥 just, simply | 두다 to leave (someone or something) | 고추 pepper

배 좌수가 그 모습을 보고 깜짝 놀랐어요. 나쁜 새엄마 때문에 힘들어진 장화, 홍련에게 미안한 마음뿐이었어요.

'정말 못된 사람이구나. 급하게 결혼하기는 했지만 앞으로의 일이 더 큰 문제겠어. 아이들 일에 이렇고 저렇고 말을 하면 체통 없다 할 것이고.'

> N + 뿐이다: An expression indicating that there is nothing other than the state or situation indicated by the preceding noun. Also used in the form "V/A + -(으)ㄹ 뿐이다."

> 체통 없다 (lit. to have no bodily appearance, dignity): Means that something isn't appropriate to one's status or position.

집에 들어와도 마음 붙일 데 없는 배 좌수는 집에 잘 안 들어오기 시작했어요. 가끔 집에 일찍

> 마음(을) 붙이다 (lit. to stick one's mind to something): To devote oneself or put one's mind to something.

들어오면 장화와 홍련의 우는 소리가 항상 들려왔어요. 배 좌수는 너무나 답답해서 허씨 부인에게 이야기했어요.

"아니, 누가 죽은 것도 아닌데 왜 이렇게 날마다 우는 소리가 나는 거요?"

"아니, 영감도. 그걸 왜 저에게 물으십니까? 무슨 말만 해도 저렇게 슬프게 웁니다. 아무래도 울음보가 터진 모양입니다. 그리고 영감, 저 애들이 언제는 안 울었습니까? 나 들어오기 전에도 항상 울었어요."

> 영감: In an older couple, a name a wife uses to call or refer to her husband.

> 울음보가 터지다 (lit. for a bunch of tears to burst): A word used to figuratively refer to crying that bursts out as you can no longer hold it.

못되다 to be bad | **급하다** to be in a rush | **항상** always | **답답하다** to be frustrated

그 말에 배 좌수는 대답하지 못했어요. 허씨 부인의 말이 틀리지 않았기 때문이었어요. 어머니가 죽은 뒤로 장화, 홍련이 잘 우는 건 사실이었어요. 그래서 배 좌수는 딸들이 우는 모습을 보고도 조용히 있을 수밖에 없었어요. 하인들 역시 허씨 부인을 멀리하였어요.

> V/A + -(으)ㄹ 밖에 없다: Indicates that there is no way or possibility other than the one mentioned.

시간이 지나 두 사람 사이에 아이가 생겼어요. 허씨 부인이 낳은 아이는 아들이었어요. 그 후로 계속해서 아들 셋을 쑥쑥 낳았어요. 배 좌수는 기다리던 아들이 태어나서 기뻐했어요.

어느 날, 허씨 부인이 없는 사이에 장화와 홍련이 안방으로 들어갔어요. 어린 동생을 한번 안아 보고 싶었어요.

"아유, 귀여워."

홍련이 아기를 조심히 안았는데 갑자기 아기가 울기 시작했어요.

"어? 아기가 왜 울지? 언니, 어떻게 해?"

"네가 안아 주는 게 불편한 것 같아. 다시 여기 놓자."

그때 방문이 열리고 허씨 부인이 화를 내며 들어왔어요.

"너희들 대체 뭐 하는 거냐?"

사실 truth | **역시** of course | **멀리하다** to avoid | **사이** between, while | **아이가 생기다** to have a child | **낳다** to bear, to give birth | **쑥쑥** smoothly, easily | **조심히** carefully | **갑자기** suddenly | **불편하다** to be uncomfortable | **놓다** to put down

"아, 어머니. 아기가 너무 예뻐서, 진짜 한 번만 안아 보려는데 갑자기……."

"아이고, 거짓말을 잘도 하는구나. 네가 괴롭혀 놓고 뭐, 갑자기 울어?"

"정말이에요, 어머니. 언니랑 저랑 진짜 한 번만 안아 보려고 했어요."

"거짓말!"

허씨 부인은 장화와 홍련에게 소리치며 화를 냈어요. 장화와 홍련이 아무리 설명해도 믿어 주지 않았어요.

"거짓말쟁이들! 여기가 어디라고 들어와?"

장화는 아무 말도 못 하고 울었고, 홍련은 "어머니, 잘못했어요." 라고 말하며 울었어요.

"나쁜 것들! 매일 울고 거짓말이나 하고! 그러니까 너희 어미가 일찍 죽었지."

> 어미: Disrespectful version of "어머니(mother)."

허씨 부인은 계속해서 아무렇지도 않게 장화와 홍련에게 나쁜 말을 했어요. 그러다 힘이 쭉 빠지자 허씨 부인은 장화와 홍련에게 나가라고 했어요. 안방에서 나온 장화와 홍련은 방으로 돌아왔어요. 어두운 방에서 자매는 '아버지는 어디에 가신 걸까? 왜 혼난 걸까?' 생각했어요. 점점 슬픈 마음이 들어 아이들은 다시 울기 시작했어요.

"엄마. 어, 엄마. 어, 어, 엄마아아아!"

거짓말 lie | 괴롭히다 to pick on, to bother | 쭉 at once, suddenly | 혼나다 to be scolded, to be yelled at

3
새어머니의 못된 거짓말

Track 03

　배 좌수도 허씨 부인의 나쁜 성격을 잘 알고 있었어요. 그러나 아들을 셋씩이나 낳아 준 허씨 부인 덕분에 대를 이을 수 있었어요. 그래서 마음에 들지 않는 일이 있어도 그냥 지나갔어요.

　장화와 홍련이 시집갈 나이가 되었어요. 배 좌수는 장화와 홍련을 볼 때마다 마음이 아프고 불쌍했어요. 먼저 간 아내 장씨에게 너무너무 미안했어요. 그래서 가끔 두 아이의 방에 가서 딸들과 엄마 이야기를 했어요.

　"아버지, 어머니 무덤에 한번 다녀오고 싶습니다."

　"그래, 어머니가 보고 싶으면 가야지. 나도 보고 싶은데."

　"아니에요, 그냥 참겠어요. 홍련이처럼 꿈속에서 어머니를 만나겠어요."

> V/A + -(으)ㄴ데: Indicates wonder, or that the speaker is waiting for the listener's reaction.

　"아니, 왜? 새어머니가 무서워서?"

　배 좌수는 허씨 부인 때문이라는 걸 알았어요.

지나가다 to pass by ｜ 무덤 tomb, grave ｜ 참다 to hold in, to surpress

"장화야, 새어머니 때문에 그렇게 말하는 걸 내가 잘 안다.
조금만 참고 지내거라. 내 중매쟁이를 구해 좋은 신랑감을 서둘러
찾아보겠다."

> 중매쟁이: A middle person who introduces people so that a marriage can take place; a matchmaker.

그 말은 돈을 많이 준비해
좋은 집으로 시집보내 주겠다는 약속이었어요. 장화와 홍련은
아버지의 말을 모두 이해했어요.

그런데 이 말을 밖에서 허씨 부인이 듣고 있었어요.

'이거 큰일이구나. 저 애들 시집보내면 이 집 돈이 반은
없어지겠구나. 그러면 내 아들들은 어떻게 되는 거지? 닭 쫓던 개 지붕
쳐다본다고, 손가락만 빠는 게
아닌가?'

> 손가락 빨다 (lit. to suck one's fingers): Indicates that a you yourself can't do anything and are only watching from the sidelines.

> TIP! 닭 쫓던 개 지붕(먼산) 쳐다보듯 (lit. staring at the roof or a distant mountain like a dog who chased the chickens): Means that something you put effort into fails or lags behind others, and there is nothing you can do about it, and comes from the meaning that when a dog chases a chicken up onto a roof, the dog can't follow it up and instead stares at the roof.

생각해 보니 이건 작은 문제가 아니었어요. 이 집의 많은
물건과 돈이 원래 장화와 홍련의 친어머니 장씨 부인이 가지고 온
것이었어요. 그러니 두 딸이 모두 가져가도 앞에서 아무 말 할 수
없었어요.

허씨 부인은 그날부터 밥을 먹지 않았어요. 잠도 잘 오지 않고
머리만 아팠어요. 몇 날 며칠을 방에 누워 생각하고 또 생각했어요.

'어떻게 하지? 어떻게 할까? 무슨 좋은 방법이 없을까?'

구하다 to look for | **신랑감** potential husband | **이해하다** to understand | **반** half | **친어머니** real mother

드디어 허씨 부인은 아주 나쁜 방법을 하나 생각해 냈어요.

'흐흐흐, 그래, 그렇게 하는 게 좋겠어. 가만! 먼저 쥐 한 마리 잡아야겠네.'

며칠 뒤, 허씨 부인이 자신의 첫째 아들 장쇠를 불러 이야기했어요.

"장쇠야, 너 쥐 잡을 줄 알지?"

"에이, 당연히 알죠. 팔뚝만 한 쥐도 손으로 잡을 수 있어요."

"그럼 너 큰 놈으로 한 마리 잡아서 이 엄마한테 가져와라."

> N + 만: Indicates the degree or extent of the preceding subject or content and is used in conjunction with 하다 or 못하다.

장쇠는 그길로 창고로 가 쥐덫을 놓고 저녁이 되기 전에 팔뚝만 한 쥐를 잡아 엄마에게 갖고 갔어요.

허씨 부인은 화장실로 가서 아무도 모르게 쥐를 죽은 아기처럼 꾸몄어요. 그리고 쥐를 천에 싸고 밤이 되기를 기다렸어요. 밤이 되자 허씨 부인이 장화와 홍련의 방으로 들어갔어요. 두 자매는 깊이 잠들어 있었어요.

'좌수 영감이 오기 전에 해야 돼. 어서 서두르자.'

허씨 부인은 장화의 이불 속에 죽은 쥐를 넣었어요. 그러고는 빨리 방을 나왔어요.

배 좌수가 일을 마치고 집으로 돌아왔어요. 허씨 부인은 일부러 배 좌수 앞에서 혀를 찼어요. 배 좌수가 이상해서 물었어요.

> 혀를 차다 (lit. to click one's tongue): Indicates a feeling of upset or regret.

쥐 rat | 마리 counter word for an animal | 당연히 of course, naturally | 팔뚝 forearm | 놈 one, thing (when talking about an animal) | 창고 storehouse | 쥐덫을 놓다 to place a rattrap | 꾸미다 to make up (to look a certain way) | 일부러 deliberately

"부인, 오늘따라 얼굴이 이상하네요. 무슨 일이 있었습니까?"

"그, 그게 저, 너무 놀라서 말이 안 나옵니다.

허씨 부인은 바로 말을 하지 않았어요.

"무슨 말을 못하겠다는 거요? 어서 말해 보시오."

"아이고, 제가 딸을 잘 가르치지 못했습니다. 어이구, 흑흑!
보나마나 영감께서는 내 말을 믿지 않으실 거고……. 앞으로 이 일을
어떡하지?"

"허허 참, 무슨 일인데 그래요? 혹시 장화와 홍련이 일이에요?"

허씨 부인은 얼른 배 좌수의 눈치를 살폈어요. 무슨 이야기를 해도
허씨 부인의 말을 다 듣겠다는

눈치를 살피다: To peep or to get a sense of someone's feelings or intentions.

얼굴이었어요. 그래서 미리
지어 놓은 말을 시작했어요.

"오늘 하루 종일 애들이 방에서 나오지 않아서 병이 났나 싶어
가 보았어요. 글쎄, 방바닥에 피가 묻어 있고 작은 살덩이가 이불
밖으로 보여서 이게 무엇이냐 물었는데요. 장화가 잠에서 일어나
나에게 화를 내서 더는 말 못 하고 나왔어요."

"그게 무슨 말입니까?"

"영감, 틀림없이 어떤 남자와 놀다가 일이 난 것 같아요."

"지금 무슨 소릴 하는 겁니까?
그럴 리가! 내 딸 장화가 그럴리
없어요!"

· V/A + -다가: A connective ending indicating that the preceding word serves as the cause or basis for the following word. ◉ 늦잠을 자다가 약속에 늦어버렸다.
· The "리" in "그럴 리가!" means "reason" or "logic," and is often used in "그럴 리가 없다." It means that a fact is hard to believe.

보나마나 obviously | 종일 all day | 방바닥 floor (of a room) | 피 blood | 살덩이 lump of flesh |
놀다 to play (around)

"흥! 영감이 내 말을 믿으면 해가 서쪽에서 뜨지요. 그래서 처음부터 내가 말하지 않겠다고 하지 않았습니까? 지금 당장 방에 가서 보고 뭐라고 하실지 궁금합니다."

> 해가 서쪽에서 뜨다 (lit. for the sun to rise in the west): Used when metaphorically expressing that something completely unexpected, or something so strange that it could never happen, is about to happen, or has happened.

배 좌수는 믿을 수 없다는 표정으로 그냥 앉아 있었어요. 하지만 이렇게 있을 수 없었어요. 배 좌수는 조심스럽게 장화의 방으로 들어갔어요. 허씨 부인의 말대로 방바닥에 피가 묻어 있었어요. 이불을 들어 보니 붉은 살덩이가 있었어요. 배 좌수는 자는 장화를 깨워 어떻게 된 일인지 물어볼 생각도 못하고 급히 문을 열고 달려 나왔어요.

"이 일을 어떻게 하면 좋을까? 으흐흑!"

이때 허씨 부인이 기다렸다는 듯이 말했어요.

"영감, 이 일이 바깥에 알려지면 좋을 게 없어요. 어린 여자가 시집도 가기 전에 아이를 낳아 죽였다고 해 보십시오. 양반 집안 체면이 무너져서 우린 이제 얼굴을 들고 살지 못합니다."

"그러면 이 일을 어떻게 하면 좋겠어요? 부인이 한번 말해 봐요."

> 얼굴을 들다 (lit. to lift one's face): Means to face other people honorably.

허씨 부인은 속으로 좋아하면서도 걱정스러운 표정으로 말했어요.

뜨다 (for the sun) to rise | 궁금하다 to be curious | 표정 expression | 조심스럽다 careful |
양반 yangban (a member of the noble class in the Joseon Dynasty), gentleman | 체면 face,
reputation | 걱정스럽다 to be worried

"장화를 보이지 않는 곳으로 멀리 떠나게 하는 수밖에 없어요."

"멀리? 어디로 말이에요?"

"사람 눈에 띄지 않는 곳이요. 눈(에) 띄다: Means to show conspicuously.
날이 밝기 전에 빨리 쥐도 새도 모르게 보내야지요."

"그런 곳이 어디에
있단 말입니까?"

쥐도 새도 모르게 (lit. without a mouse or a bird knowing):
Means to act or deal with something so inconspicuously
that nobody knows its whereabouts.

"북망산이요!"

"부, 북망산?"

북망산 (Mt. Bukmangsan): A word used to refer to a place with
a lot of graves or where a lot of dead people are buried, and
is used with the meaning of a place you go when you die.

"네, 영감. 이 말을 하면 계모가 전처 자식을 죽이려 한다고
하겠지만 다른 방법이 없어요. 그렇지 않으면 우리 모두 죽어야
합니다. 양반 체면이고 뭐고 다 무너질 것입니다. 그러니 죽은
목숨이나 마찬가지 아니겠습니까?"

"그, 그건 그렇지만, 그래도 어찌 산 자식을……. 좀 더 좋은 생각
없겠어요?"

"생각해 보았어요. 그렇지만 살아도 죽을 때까지 부끄럽게 살아야
하고, 만약 이 일이 알려지면 다른 자식 결혼도 못 할 것이니! 그러니
영감, 빨리 정하셔야 합니다."

생각할수록 허씨 부인의 말이 맞는 것 같았어요. 어쩔 수 없이
배 좌수는 부인의 말대로 하기로 했어요.

떠나다 to leave | 계모 stepmother | 전처 former wife | 목숨 life | 마찬가지 the same |
정하다 to decide

4

억울하게 죽임을 당하는 장화

Track 04

　허씨 부인은 장쇠를 불러 말을 준비시키고 조용히 무언가를 말했어요. 그리고 장화를 깨우러 갔어요.

　장화는 이상한 소리를 듣고 놀라 눈을 떴어요. 밖에서 장화를 부르는 소리였어요.

　"장화야, 일어나라."

　"네? 아, 네, 어머니!"

　허씨 부인이 부르는 것을 들은 장화는 일어나 바깥으로 나왔어요.

　"네 외할머니께서 급히 너를 부르신다. 네 어머니 대신 너를 보고 싶어 하신다. 지금 곧 장쇠를 따라 네 외갓집으로 가야겠구나."

　"지, 지금 당장요?"

　"그래, 어서 급히 가야 한다. 장쇠가 너를 데려다줄 거야."

　장화 생각에 무언가 좋지 않은 일이 생긴 것 같았어요. 그래서 옷을 갈아입고 나오겠다고 하고는 다시 방으로 들어가 홍련을 깨웠어요.

깨우다 to wake up | 외할머니 maternal grandmother | 외갓집 maternal grandparents' house |
데려다주다 to take someone somewhere

"홍련아, 언니는 외갓집에 가야 한다."

"외갓집에? 왜?"

"나도 모른다. 어서 빨리 가야 한다고 하시는데…… 널 혼자 두고 가려니 역시 불안하구나. 우리 서로 옷을 바꿔 입자. 혹시라도 언니가 보고 싶으면 이 옷을 보면서 언니를 생각하면 돼. 알았지?"

"언니, 가지 마! 아버지께 말씀드려서 안 간다고 해. 응?"

"안 돼. 괜찮을 거야. 외할머니가 부르시니까 빨리 다녀올게. 잘 있어, 홍련아."

장화는 서둘러 옷을 입고 밖으로 나왔어요. 어둠 속에 서 있는 아버지의 모습이 보였어요. 장화가 고개 숙여 인사를 하자 장쇠가 말과 함께 나타났어요.

"빨리 타요. 누나 때문에 잠도 못 자고 이게 무슨 일입니까?"

장쇠는 장화를 말에 태우고 집 밖으로 나왔어요.

가도 가도 길은 안 나오고 깊은 산 속으로 계속 들어갔어요. 산짐승들의 울음소리가 계속 들려와서 무서웠어요.

> V/A + -아/어도 V/A + -아/어도:
> Indicates that what follows is out of step with what you expect from the preceding fact or supposition.

"장쇠야, 무섭구나. 외갓집으로 가는 길이 맞는 거야?"

"아이, 누나만 무서운 줄 알아요? 나도 무서워요. 그러니 조용히 갑시다."

불안하다 to be anxious | **서두르다** to hurry | **고개를 숙이다** to bow one's head | **태우다** to (have someone) ride (something), to give someone a ride | **산짐승** wild animals (in the mountains) | **울음소리** crying sound

장쇠는 그렇게 말하고 더욱 깊은 숲으로 들어갔어요. 어두운 숲에서 흐르는 물소리가 귀신 울음소리처럼 들렸어요.

드디어 깊은 산속에 연못이 나타났어요. 그 연못은 아주 깊어 보였어요. 그런데 갑자기 장쇠가 연못가에 말을 세웠어요.

"누나, 여기서 그만 내려요."

"아, 아니, 자, 장쇠야. 이 어두운 연못가에 내리라고?"

"내리면 얘기해 줄게요."

장쇠는 장화가 말에서 내릴 때까지 기다렸어요.

"누나는 해서는 안 되는 아주 부끄러운 일을 했어요. 어머니가 말씀하셨어요. 누나는 그 죗값으로 스스로 목숨을 버려야 한다고요. 나는 여기까지 그 길을 안내해 주러 온 것입니다. 외갓집에 간다는 말은 거짓말입니다."

> 목숨을 버리다 (lit. to throw away one's life): Means to kill oneself.

"뭐, 뭐라고? 내가 언제? 어디서? 뭘, 어떻게 했다는 거야?"

"아니, 누나. 왜 나에게 화를 내십니까? 시집도 가기 전에 아이를 낳고도 부끄럽지 않습니까?"

"어떻게 그런 말을!"

"어머니, 아버지도 다 아시는 일입니다."

숲 woods, forest | 어둡다 to be dark | 귀신 ghost | 연못 pond | 연못가 pondside (the area beside a pond) | 세우다 to (bring something to a) stop | 죗값 price for one's crime

"장쇠야, 아니다. 그건 아니야. 그런 말도 안 되는 일을!"

"자, 그만 말하고 서두르십시오. 누나 때문에 가족들 모두 얼굴을 들고 살 수 없게 되었으니, 스스로 목숨을 버리십시오."

어서 연못 속으로 빠져 죽으라는 말을 장쇠는 눈썹 하나 까딱 않고 말하는 것이었어요.

> 눈썹 하나 까딱하지 않다 (lit. to not move an eyebrow): Expresses that not only is a person not surprised, they appear very calm.

그제야 장화는 새어머니가 자신을 죽이려고 한 것을 알고 바닥에 앉아 울기 시작했어요.

"오, 하늘이여! 어떻게 저에게 이렇게 나쁜 일만 생깁니까? 이대로 죽으면 제 억울한 마음은 누가 알아주시나요? 불쌍한 우리 홍련이는 누가 지켜 준단 말입니까?"

> N + 이여: A particle that primarily denotes polite summons, often expressing admiration or appeal.

장화의 말이 산 깊은 곳까지 울렸어요. 그런데도 장쇠는 귀찮다는 듯 서서 하품만 하고 있었어요.

"여기까지 온 거, 빨리 합시다. 안 그러면 산짐승에게 물려 죽을 수도 있다고요. 그리고 나도 어서 가서 자고 싶습니다. 한밤중에 이게 무슨 일입니까? 졸려 죽겠어요."

> Adj + -아/어 죽다: Expresses that the degree of the emotion or state indicated by the adjective is very severe.

장화는 동생에게 부탁했어요. 멀리 가서 다시는 안 나타나겠으니 살려 달라고 했어요. 하지만 장쇠는 서두르라고 자꾸 화를 냈어요.

빠져 죽다 to drown | 그제야 only then | 억울하다 to feel unfair or unjust | 울리다 to ring out, to resound | 귀찮다 to be a bother, to be annoyed | 하품 yawn | 물리다 to be bitten | 한밤중 the middle of the night | 살리다 to save sb's life, to keep sb alive

장화는 무서워서 몸을 떨며 신발을 벗었어요. 눈물을 흘리며
장쇠에게 마지막 부탁을 했어요.

"장쇠야, 나는 이렇게 하지도 않은
일 때문에 억울하게 먼저 가지만
불쌍한 우리 홍련이를 잘 부탁한다.

TIP! 신발을 벗다 (to take off one's shoes): The act of taking off one's shoes has a meaning of leaving this world. In Korea, there is a culture of taking off one's shoes when entering a certain space. It's said that you take off your shoes with the meaning that after you die, you go to another place, and there are also opinions that it's done regret, in the hopes that people in this world will find you.

오, 불쌍한 홍련아! 내가 너를 두고 먼저 가서 미안하다."

그리고 나서 장화는 쓰개치마를 머리에 쓰고 연못 속으로 '풍덩'
뛰어들었어요.

쓰개치마 (lit. a headpiece skirt or covering skirt): A skirt worn by women in the past to cover the face and upper part of the body when leaving the house.

떨다 to shake, to tremble | 눈물을 흘리다 for tears to flow, to cry | 부탁 favor, request |
풍덩 sploosh (the sound made when a large, heavy object falls or plunges into deep water)

바로 그때였어요. '어흥!' 소리와 함께 큰 호랑이가 나타났어요.

"억! 아! 호, 호, 호랑이다!"

장쇠는 무서워서 도망을 치려고 해도 발이 땅에 붙어서 떨어지지
않았어요.

"어흥! 나쁜 놈이구나. 그 어미에 그 아들! 네 이놈! 불쌍하고 착한
네 누나를 죽게 하다니! 너 또한 가만두지 않겠다. 어흥!"

그리고 장쇠의 귀와 팔과 다리 하나씩을 물어뜯어 버렸어요.
장쇠는 피를 흘리며 그대로 정신을 잃었어요. 놀란 말은 바로 집으로
돌아갔어요.

> 정신을 잃다 (lit. to lose consciousness): Means to faint out of fear, surprise, shock, etc.

허씨 부인이 아무리
기다려도 장쇠가 오지 않았어요. 말만 집으로 와서 무슨 일이 생긴 것
같았어요. 집안 하인들을 보내 장쇠를 찾게 하였어요. 하인들이 한쪽
팔다리가 없어진 장쇠를 연못가에서 찾아왔어요. 허씨 부인은 급히
장쇠의 상처를 치료하고 약을 지어 먹였어요. 배 좌수는 호랑이에게
물려서 다친 장쇠를 보고 무서웠어요. 뭔가 일이 잘못됐다는 생각이
들었어요.

'호랑이가 물어뜯다니! 하늘이 화나신 거야. 그렇다면 장화는
어떻게 된 거지?'

어흥 the sound of a lion or tiger roaring | 호랑이 tiger | 도망을 치다 to run away | 땅 the ground |
붙다 to stick (to something) | 가만두다 to leave alone | 씩 each | 물어뜯다 to bite off |
상처를 치료하다 to treat (someone's) wounds

5

언니를 따라 연못에 뛰어든 홍련

Track 05

"언니! 언니! 혼자 어디 가는 거야?"

홍련이 울며 말했어요. 장화가 뒤를 돌아보며 눈물을 흘리며 말했어요.

"홍련아, 미안하다. 너와 나의 길은 서로 달라. 나는 지금 너무 바빠서 오래 말할 수가 없구나. 하지만 곧 너를 데리러 올게. 조금만 기다려."

장화의 말이 끝나고 홍련은 깜짝 놀라 일어났어요. 꿈이었어요. 너무나 기억에 남는 꿈!

'이상한 꿈이구나. 언니에게 무슨 일이 생긴 게 틀림없어.'

홍련은 용기를 내어 아버지에게 물었어요.

"아버지, 오늘도 꿈에 언니를 보았어요. 외갓집에 다녀온다던 언니는 오지 않고 자꾸 꿈에 나타나 울기만 하니 무슨 일이 생긴 것이 틀림없어요."

배 좌수는 홍련의 말을 듣고 숨이 막히는 것 같았어요. 그리고 아무 말도 없이 눈물만 흘렸어요.

> 숨이 막히다: An expression used when feeling so stifled that you can't breathe, or when a certain situation is making you feel seriously nervous or pressured.

기억에 남다 to stay in one's memory | 용기를 내다 to gather one's courage

"영감, 무슨 일입니까? 홍련이 너는 또 무슨 말로 네 아버지
마음을 아프게 했어? 어서 나가지 못해?"

갑자기 허씨 부인이 뛰어 들어와서 홍련에게 소리를 질렀어요.
새어머니의 말에 홍련은 아버지 방에서 나왔어요. 홍련은 언니가
너무 보고 싶어서 그만 병이 났어요. 그리고 그대로 자리에 눕고
말았어요. 그런데 허씨 부인은 혼자
남은 홍련을 더욱 못 살게 했어요.

> 자리에 눕다 (lit. to lie down in one's place): Means "to be bedridden with illness" or "to get sick."

허씨 부인이 밖에 나간 어느 날, 며칠째 아무것도 먹지 못한
홍련은 겨우 일어났어요. 그리고 장쇠를 불러 장화에게 무슨 일이
있었는지 묻고 또 물었어요. 장쇠는 드디어 장화의 일을 말했어요.
이야기를 다 듣고 난 홍련은 그만 자리에 주저앉았어요.

'그랬구나! 그래서 언니가 슬프게 울었던 거구나. 새어머니가
아버지에게 거짓말을 해서 언니를 죽게 만들었구나!'

홍련은 슬퍼서 눈물을 흘렸어요. 언니와 함께 놀던 뒷마당, 함께
썼던 이불과 머리빗만 보아도 눈물이 나왔어요.

'언니, 정말 너무해. 나만 놔두고 가다니. 나도 데려가……'

소리를 지르다 to shout | 째 suffix indicating a period of time or an order | 겨우 barely, with great
difficulty | 주저앉다 to drop, to sink | 뒷마당 backyard | 머리빗 comb, hair brush | 놔두다 to leave
(something or someone) alone/aside

더 이상 살고 싶지 않은 홍련은 자신도 언니를 따라 죽어야겠다고 생각했어요. 하지만 집 밖을 돌아다녀 본 적 없는 홍련은 언니가 죽은 연못을 찾아갈 수 없었어요.

> V + -(으)ㄴ 적이 있다/없다: Indicates whether or not one has had an experience in the past.

그러던 어느 날 밤, 홍련이 방문을 열어 놓고 앉아 있을 때 파랑새 한 마리가 꽃밭으로 날아왔어요. 이 꽃 저 꽃을 옮겨 다니며 꽃밭을 떠나지 않았어요. 너무 이상해서 홍련이 밖으로 나와 파랑새를 쫓아갔어요.

'혹시 언니가 파랑새로 변해서 온 게 아닐까?'

그런 생각을 한 홍련이 파랑새에게 부탁했어요.

"파랑새야, 너는 우리 언니가 있는 곳을 알고 있니? 안다면 나에게도 좀 알려 줘."

그러자 홍련의 말을 알아들은 것처럼 파랑새가 고개를 끄덕이는 게 아니겠어요? 그러더니 조금씩 앞서 날아갔어요. 홍련은 소리가 안 나게 조용히 대문을 열고 집 밖으로 나갔어요.

파랑새가 빙빙 돌며 앞서 날아갔어요. 그리고 다시 돌아오고 또 앞서갔다가 다시 돌아왔어요. 홍련에게 길을 안내하였어요. 홍련은 파랑새를 따라 마을을 나왔어요. 풀밭을 지나 숲속으로 들어갔어요.

파랑새 blue bird | **꽃밭** flower garden | **쫓아가다** to chase after | **끄덕이다** to nod | **앞서다** to be ahead | **날아가다** to fly (away) | **대문** front gate | **빙빙** in circles, round and round | **풀밭** meadow, grass

해가 지고 밤이 되었어요. 홍련은 무지개가 떠 있는 어느 연못에
도착하였어요. 그런데 갑자기 파랑새가 연못을 돌며 슬프게
울었어요.

'아, 여기로구나. 언니가 이곳에 있구나. 나도 저곳으로 들어가야지.'

홍련은 눈물을 흘리면서 연못을 바라보았어요. 그런데 바로 그때,
안개 속에서 슬픈 여자 목소리가 들려왔어요.

"홍련아! 홍련아아아아!"

"어, 언니? 언니? 장화 언니!"

홍련이 반갑게 소리쳤어요.

"그래, 홍련아. 어서 와. 내가 너에게 꼭 할 말이 있어서 파랑새를
보냈어. 내 말 잘 들어. 사람은 한번 죽으면 다시 살아나지 못해.
목숨은 소중한 거야. 그러니 어서 집으로 돌아가. 제발 부탁이야,
홍련아."

"싫어, 언니. 난 언니 없는 세상에서 더 살 수 없어. 나도 언니랑
함께 가고 싶어. 언니가 억울하게 죽었을 때 나도 더 이상 살고 싶지
않았어. 오, 하느님! 저도 언니를 따라갑니다. 우리 언니 억울함만
풀어 주세요."

해가 지다 for the sun to set | 무지개 rainbow, moonbow | 뜨다 to float | 살아나다 to survive,
to come back to life | 소중하다 to be precious | 하느님 god

울면서 말하던 홍련이 벌떡 일어나서 하늘을 향해 큰절을 올리고는 치마를 머리에 쓰고 물속으로 뛰어들었어요.

큰절을 올리다: The act of a person of lower standing bowing politely. Here, this expression indicates the behavior of giving a final greeting with the meaning of a daughter apologizing for ending her life before her parent.

"홍련아! 홍련아아아아!"

"흐흐흐흑! 언니이이이!"

그 뒤로 이 울음소리는 그치지 않았어요. 밤낮으로 연못가에 우는 소리가 들렸어요. 숲에 들어온 사람이나 이 길을 지나는 사람이면 누구나 이 소리를 들을 수 있었어요.

벌떡 describes the motion of suddenly rising from a lying or sitting position | **그치다** to stop

6

자매의 억울함을 풀어 주는 사또

Track 06

그런데 이상한 일이 생기기 시작했어요. 철산에 농사가 잘되지 않아서 밥을 못 먹어 죽는 사람이 많아졌어요. 점점 마을에 사람이 줄어서 나라에서 새로운 사또를 보냈어요. 그런데 새로 오는 사또마다 하룻밤도 지내지 못하고 죽는 일이 계속 있었어요.

왕도 이 사실을 알고 걱정이 많았어요.

"철산에 이런 일이 일어나는데, 누가 그곳에 내려가 백성들을 도와주겠습니까?"

신하들 중에 아무도 가려는 사람이 없었어요. 신하들은 튼튼하고 정직한 데에다가 무척이나 용기 있는 정동우를 추천했어요. 정동우를 본 왕이 크게 기뻐했어요.

> N + 에다가: Used to add something else onto another object or situation.

"철산에서 일어나는 일 때문에 백성들의 어려움이 큽니다. 빨리 그곳으로 가서 소문이 사실인지 알아보고 백성들의 마음을 편하게 해 주세요!"

농사 farming | 줄다 to decrease | 사또 satto (a title used by commoners or minor officials when adressing a magistrate in Joseon Dynasty) | 하룻밤 one night | 내려가다 to go down to | 백성 the people | 신하 vassal | 정직하다 to be honest | 추천하다 to recommend | 편하다 to be at ease

정동우는 그날로 철산으로 내려갔어요. 마을에 도착해서 이방을 불러 지금까지의 일을 자세히 물어보았어요.

"이방! 이곳에 온 사또들마다 하룻밤을 못 보내고 죽었다는데 그 말이 사실입니까?"

"네, 그렇습니다. 말씀드리기 좀 그렇지만 모두 하루 만에 죽었습니다. 그러나 지금까지 그 이유를 알지 못합니다."

사또는 눈을 감고 생각했어요. 그리고 관청의 부하들을 불러 말했어요.

"너희는 오늘 밤에 잠을 자지 마라. 정신을 차리고 무슨 일이 생기는지 살펴보아라."

> 관청: An institution that carries out affairs of the nation, and is divided into administrative and judicial offices according to the nature of those affairs, as well as into central and local offices, depending on the region; A government office.

> 정신을 차리다 (lit. to regain consciousness): Means to stay awake and keep your mind clear.

사또는 불을 밝게 켜고 책을 읽기 시작했어요. 깊은 밤, 사또는 점점 졸렸어요. 그런데 갑자기 찬 바람이 불면서 불이 꺼졌어요.

사또는 정신을 차리고 똑바로 앉아 있었어요. 그런데 그때, 갑자기 어떤 여자가 나타나 조용히 절을 하는 것이었어요.

이방 yibang (a frontline provincial official in charge of personnel and secretarial affairs during the Joseon Dynasty) | 부하 subordinate | 밝다 to be bright | 꺼지다 (for a light) to go out | 똑바로 upright, straight | 절을 하다 to bow

"너, 너는 누구냐? 귀신이냐? 사람이냐?"

사또가 큰 소리로 말했어요. 그러자 하얀 한복을 입은 여자가 일어나 한 번 더 절을 하였어요.

"사또, 늦은 밤에 갑자기 찾아와서 죄송합니다. 저는 철산 좌수 배무용의 딸, 홍련이라고 합니다. 그런데 너무도 억울한 일로 죽게 되어 이렇게 찾아왔어요."

> V/A + -게 되다: Indicates that a certain result occurs or a situation or state changes because a situation is influenced externally.

그 귀신은 언니를 따라 스스로 목숨을 끊었던 홍련이었어요. 홍련은 자신의 집에서 생긴 일들을 자세히 이야기했어요. 사또는 무서워하지 않고 가만히 앉아 홍련의 이야기를 모두 들었어요. 말을 마친 홍련은 일어나 절을 하고 갔어요.

놀란 사또는 아침까지 잠을 잘 수가 없었어요.

'철산이 이렇게 된 것이 혹시 이 일 때문이 아닐까?'

다음날 아침 일찍 사또는 관청으로 나갔어요. 하룻밤이 지났는데 죽지 않고 나타난 사또를 보고 사람들이 모두 깜짝 놀랐어요. 사또는 이 마을에 배무용이라는 좌수가 있는지 이방에게 물었어요.

"네, 있습니다. 죽은 부인의 재산으로 잘 산다고 들었습니다."

"그럼 새 부인을 얻었다는 말이군요. 자식은 몇 명입니까?"

"죽은 부인에게서 얻은 두 딸은 죽고 새 부인에게서 얻은 아들 셋이 있습니다."

가만히 still

"두 딸은 왜 죽었습니까?"

"소문으로는 큰딸은 죄를 짓고 연못에 빠져 죽었는데, 언니의 죽음을 알고 동생도 슬퍼서 울다가 따라 죽었다고 합니다. 그 뒤로 그 연못을 지날 때면, 두 여자의 슬픈 울음소리가 들려 사람들이 그곳을 지나갈 때 무서워합니다."

이방의 말을 들은 사또는 곧 배 좌수와 허씨 부인을 불렀어요. 관청의 부하들에게 잡혀 온 두 사람에게 사또가 장화와 홍련의 일을 물었어요. 배 좌수는 떨며 대답했어요.

"이미 알고 물으시는데 어떻게 거짓말을 하겠습니까."

배 좌수는 홍련까지 집을 나갔기 때문에 누구에게 말도 못 하고 혼자 답답해하고 있었어요. 배 좌수는 장화가 아이를 낳은 이야기를 천천히 시작했어요.

"그럼 아이를 낳았다는 증거를 가져와 보아라."

허씨 부인이 작은 천을 꺼내 사또에게 보여 주며 말했어요.

"아이고, 사또. 그 물건이라면 제가 가지고 왔어요. 너무 놀라 그것을 버리지 못하고 이렇게 갖고 있었어요."

죄를 짓다 to commit a crime or sin | 증거 proof | 천 cloth

사또는 그 물건을 보고 머리가 복잡해졌어요.

"그럼 내가 좀 더 알아본 뒤에 다시 부르겠다. 오늘은 그만 가라."

계속 시끄럽게 말을 하며 나가는 허씨 부인을 바라보며 사또는 화가 났어요.

'아무리 새어머니라지만 너무하는군. 양반인데도 체면을 생각하지 않고 딸의 잘못을 너무 쉽게 이야기하는구나! 그런데 어젯밤 그 여자는 무엇이 억울하다는 거지?
이렇게 잘못한 증거까지 있는데…….
하지만 이상해…….'

> V/A + -(는)구나: Used to draw attention to how that the speaker has seen or heard a new fact. In particular, used when speaking to oneself, a person of lower standing, or a close friend, with a meaning of wonder.

그리고 밤이 되었을 때, 찬바람이 불면서 어젯밤 그 여자가 다시 찾아왔어요. 이번에는 장화와 홍련이 함께 나타나 사또에게 절을 하였어요. 그리고 울며 부탁하였어요.

"사또, 저희 새어머니는 거짓말을 하고 있습니다. 내일은 그 죽은 아기를 다시 보자 해서 아기의 배를 열어 보십시오. 그래서 우리의 억울함을 풀어 주시고 새어머니와 장쇠에게 벌을 주십시오. 하지만 저희 아버지는 용서해 주세요. 아내를 잘못 만나서 거짓말에 속았던 것입니다."

복잡하다 to be complicated, to be complex | **벌을 주다** to punish | **용서하다** to forgive | **속다** to deceive

그때 문이 열리고 푸른 학이 나타났어요. 말을 끝낸 두 자매는
학을 타고 날아갔어요.

"내가 반드시 두 사람의 억울함을 풀어 주어야겠다."

푸르다 to be vivid blue (like a deep ocean, clear sky, etc.) | 학 crane (bird) | 반드시 must, certainly

7

나쁜 사람들의 결말

Track 07

다음날 아침이 되었어요. 사또는 다시 배 좌수와 허씨 부인을 불렀어요. 그리고 그 죽은 아기를 다시 가져오라고 했어요.

"이것이 죽은 아기라는 말이지?"

"네, 그렇습니다. 사또."

"만약 거짓말이라면 어떻게 되는지는 알고 있겠지?"

사또는 허씨 부인이 보는 앞에서 죽은 아기의 배를 열어 보라고 말했어요.

"자, 모두 잘 보세요. 이것이 무엇인가요?"

허씨 부인이 그만 놀라서 뒤로 넘어졌어요. 배 좌수는 떨며 울기 시작했어요. 옆에 서 있던 관청의 부하들도 보고 놀라 소리쳤어요.

"아니, 이건 쥐똥, 쥐똥이잖아! 세상에 이런 나쁜 사람이 있을까?"

"얼른 두 사람의 목에 칼을 채워라! 그리고 두 사람은 모든 사실을 자세히 얘기해라!"

> The 칼 in "목에 칼을 채우다" is an instrument used for punishment with the same function as today's handcuffs. In the past, in order to hold a criminal, their neck was put in a 칼.

쥐똥 rat droppings

배 좌수는 크게 슬퍼하며 울기 시작했어요. 잠시 후 울음을 그치고 이야기를 꺼냈어요.

"장화와 홍련의 어머니 장씨는 매우 착하고 훌륭한 사람이었어요. 그러나 아들 없이 두 딸을 두고 먼저 세상을 떠났어요. 삼년상을 치른 후 대를 잇기 위해 튼튼한 새 부인을 구했습니다. 성격이 나빠 보였지만 두 딸과 잘 지냈으면 했습니다. 그런데 하루는 저에게 말했는데……."

"그래, 무슨 말을 했지?"

"네, 사또. 부인이 저에게 말했어요. 자신이 새엄마라 말하지 못했는데 장화에게 큰일이 났다고요. 처음에 믿지 않았지만 딸의 이불에 피가 묻어 있었고 정말 아이를 낳은 것처럼 보였어요. 그래서 그만……."

사또가 이번에는 허씨 부인에게 물었어요. 하지만 허씨 부인은 끝까지 자기 잘못이 없다고 말했어요. 관청의 하인들이 허씨를 틀에 묶고 매를 때렸어요. 결국에 허씨 부인은 사실을 말했어요.

"사또, 장화가 죽은 것은 제 잘못입니다. 시집갈 때, 집에 많은 물건과 돈을 다 가져갈 것 같아서, 그러면 제 아들들한테 아무것도 주지 못해서 그랬어요. 용서받지 못할 죄를 지었어요. 다만 제 아들 장쇠는 이미 호랑이에게 벌을 받았으니, 아들만은 살려 주십시오."

이야기를 꺼내다 to begin to tell a story, to bring up something | **훌륭하다** to be wonderful, to be remarkable | **틀에 묶다** to tie to a frame | **매를 때리다** to whip, to lash

　그래도 허씨 부인은 장쇠의 어머니라고, 자식만은 살려 달라고
부탁했어요.

　"그럼 동생 홍련은 어떻게 되었지?"

　"호, 홍련은 어, 어디론가 사라져 버린 뒤 아… 아직 소식이
없어요."

　"매우 나쁜 사람이구나! 홍련 또한 자기 언니를 따라 죽었다.
잘 알고 있잖아!"

사라지다 to disappear ｜ 소식 news

허씨는 너무 무서워서 아무 말도 못 했어요. 사또는 허씨는 물론 그 아들 장쇠에게도 칼을 씌웠어요.

> 칼을 씌우다: Means to put a criminal's neck in the hole of a 칼.

그리고 왕에게 알렸어요.

사또는 못된 허씨 부인과 장쇠를 죽이고 배 좌수의 목숨은 살려 주었어요.

며칠 뒤 사또는 관청의 부하들과 함께 장화와 홍련이 죽은 연못으로 갔어요. 바람 소리가 두 자매의 울음소리처럼 들렸어요. 하인들을 시켜 그 연못의 물을 며칠 동안 다 퍼내게 했어요. 드디어 연못 가장 깊은 곳에서 죽은 두 자매를 찾았어요. 오랫동안 물속에 있었는데도 두 자매는 살아 있을 때랑 똑같았어요. 사람들은 모두 놀랐어요.

"저것 좀 보세요! 어떻게 저렇게 깨끗할 수가 있습니까?"

사또는 두 자매의 옷을 갈아입혔어요. 관에 눕힌 다음 두 자매의 억울한 이야기를 적어서 사람들에게

> 관: Means a wooden box that contains a dead body; a coffin.

알려 주었어요.

그리고 햇빛이 잘 비치는 산에 무덤을 만들고 비석을 세웠어요.

사또가 잠시 눈을 붙이려고 누웠는데 갑자기 장화와 홍련이 나타나 큰절을 하였어요.

> 눈(을) 붙이다 (lit. to stick one's eyes together): Means to sleep.

퍼내다 to draw (water), to scoop | 햇빛이 비치다 for the sunlight to shine | 비석을 세우다 to put up a tombstone

"사또, 우리의 억울함을 풀어 주시고 물속에서 꺼내어 주셔서 감사합니다. 그리고 우리 아버지의 죄를 용서해 주셔서 정말 감사합니다. 사또께서는 곧 높은 벼슬에 오르시게 될 것입니다. 사또, 우리 자매는 이만 갑니다. 안녕히 계십시오."

사또가 눈을 뜨자 모든 것이 그대로였어요.

"아! 억울함이 풀린 자매가 나에게 인사를 하려고 왔었구나!"

그 후 사또는 더 높은 벼슬에 올라서 나중에 장군까지 되었어요.

장화, 홍련의 아버지 배 좌수는 혼자 남아 두 딸을 그리워하며 살았어요. 그런 배 좌수를 불쌍하게 생각한 마을 사람들이 윤 씨 집안의 딸을 소개해 주었어요. 둘은 결혼하여 장화와 홍련을 꼭 닮은 쌍둥이 딸을 얻었어요.

> 장군: Refers to a position that leads and commands soldiers as the head of an army; a general.

그래서 이름도 다시 장화와 홍련이라 지었어요. 그 쌍둥이 딸을 사랑으로 키워 장원급제한 쌍둥이 형제와 결혼시켰어요. 그리고 모두 즐겁고 행복하게 살았어요.

> In the past, "장원급제" meant to pass the test used to choose administrators in first place, which can be compared to coming in first place in the current exam for choosing civil servants.

오르다 to go up, to ascend | 그대로 as something is (without changing) | 이름을 짓다 to name (someone)

부록
Appendix

1

1 빈칸에 알맞은 단어를 넣어 문장을 완성하세요.

Complete the sentences by filling in the blanks with the correct words.

자매	태몽	쌍둥이	눈을 뜨다	기도하다

(1) 장씨 부인이 자다가 깜짝 놀라 (　　　　　　)았/었어요.

(2) 배 좌수는 장씨 부인의 꿈이 (　　　　)(이)라고 했어요.

(3) 장씨 부인은 자식이 없어서 매일 (　　　　　)았/었어요.

(4) 어머니를 잃은 장화와 홍련 (　　　　　)의 슬픔은 더 깊어졌어요.

(5) 장화와 홍련은 세 살 차이지만 (　　　　　)처럼 늘 함께 있었어요.

2 아래에서 알맞은 것을 골라 '-(으)면서'를 사용해서 둘 이상의 행동을 동시에 함을 뜻하는 문장을 완성하세요.

Choose the correct words from the following and use "-(으)면서" to complete the sentences to mean that 2 or more actions occur at the same time.

듣다	굽다	마시다	읽다	열다

(1) 책을 (　　　　　) 점심을 먹어요.

(2) 창문을 (　　　　　) 밖을 봤어요.

(3) 보통 음악을 (　　　　　　) 공부해요.

(4) 빵을 (　　　　　) 과자도 같이 만들었어요.

(5) 커피를 (　　　　　) 이야기하는 사람이 하늘 씨예요.

3 다음 중 '-(으)로'의 의미가 나머지와 <u>다른</u> 것은 무엇입니까?

Which of the following uses "-(으)로" with a <u>different</u> meaning from the other options?

① 제 동생은 학교에서 반장으로 뽑혔어요.

② 저는 생일 축하 카드를 보통 손으로 직접 써요.

③ 그 사람은 인간으로 해서는 안 되는 일을 했다.

④ 에릭 씨는 한국 학교에서 영어 선생님으로 일해요.

4 장화와 홍련이라는 이름의 뜻은 무엇입니까?

What are the meanings of the names Janghwa and Hongryeon?

(1) 장화: _____ (이)라는 뜻

(2) 홍련: _____ (이)라는 뜻

5 누가 한 말입니까? 알맞게 연결하세요.

Who said this? Connect the correct answers.

(1) "제가 죽으면 우리 두 딸을 잘 부탁해요." •

· ①

배 좌수

(2) "왜 그런 말을 하세요?
    걱정하지 말고 얼른 일어나세요." •

· ②

장씨 부인

(3) "저에게 예쁜 아기 하나만 보내 주세요." •

6 다음 중 장씨 부인과 관련이 <u>없는</u> 것은 무엇입니까?

Which of the following <u>does not</u> apply to Lady Jang?

① 남편에게 마지막 부탁을 하고 눈을 감았습니다.

② 꿈속에서 선녀가 준 꽃을 받고 딸을 낳았습니다.

③ 40살이 다 되어 갈 때까지 아이를 낳지 못했습니다.

④ 좋은 약을 다 써 봤지만 병이 점점 더 심각해졌습니다.

2

1 빈칸에 알맞은 단어를 넣어 문장을 완성하세요.

Complete the sentences by filling in the blanks with the correct words.

마음에 걸리다	키우다	코끼리	사이	거짓말

(1) 아이고, 넌 (   )을/를 잘도 하는구나.

(2) 배 좌수와 허씨 부인 (   )에 아이가 생겼어요.

(3) 배 좌수는 장씨 부인의 말이 (   )았/었어요.

(4) 허씨는 허리가 굵고 다리는 (   ) 다리 같았어요.

(5) 우리 딸들을 잘 (   )아/어/여 줄 수 있는 사람이면 좋겠습니다.

2 아래의 단어와 '-(으)ㄹ 수밖에 없다'를 사용해서 그것 말고는 다른 방법이나 가능성이 없음을 뜻하는 문장을 완성하세요.

Choose the correct words from the following and use "-(으)ㄹ 수밖에 없다" to complete the sentences to mean that there is no other way or possibility.

있다	공부하다	배우다	먹다	걷다

(1) 너무 슬프지만 지금은 조용히 (   )아/어요.

(2) 자고 싶지만 내일 시험이 있으니까 (   )아/어요.

(3) 여기서부터는 차가 지나갈 수 없는 곳이라서 (   )아/어요.

(4) 한국어가 좀 어렵지만 전공이기 때문에 열심히 (   )아/어요.

(5) 저는 매운 음식을 싫어하지만 매운 음식만 있는 곳에서는 (   )아/어요.

3   **다음 중 그 뜻이 <u>다른</u> 것은 무엇입니까?**

Which of the following has a <u>different</u> meaning?

① 장씨 부인이 삼 년 후에 떠났어요.

② 장씨 부인이 삼 년 전에 떠났어요.

③ 장씨 부인이 떠난 지 삼 년이 됐어요.

④ 장씨 부인이 떠나고 삼 년이 지났어요.

4   **글의 내용과 같은 것은 무엇입니까?**

Which is correct according to the story?

① 허씨 부인은 장화와 홍련 때문에 매일 울었습니다.

② 장화와 홍련은 어린 동생이 귀엽다고 생각했습니다.

③ 배 좌수는 허씨 부인의 모든 것이 마음에 들었습니다.

④ 허씨 부인은 하인들 대신 장화와 홍련에게 일을 시켰습니다.

5   **배 좌수가 집에 안 들어오기 시작한 이유는 무엇입니까?**

What is the reason that Bae Jwasu stopped coming home?

_____

6   **허씨 부인이 아기와 함께 있던 장화와 홍련에게 화를 낸 이유는 무엇입니까?**

What is the reason that Lady Heo got angry with Janghwa and Hongryeon, who were with the baby?

_____

3

1 빈칸에 알맞은 단어를 넣어 문장을 완성하세요.

Complete the sentences by filling in the blanks with the correct words.

무덤	친어머니	뜨다	떠나다	이해하다

(1) 장화와 홍련의 ( )은/는 장씨 부인이다.

(2) 해는 동쪽에서 ( )아/어서 서쪽에서 진다.

(3) 장화와 홍련은 아버지의 말을 모두 ( )았/었다.

(4) 허씨 부인은 장화를 집에서 멀리 ( )게 하려고 했다.

(5) 장화와 홍련은 어머니의 ( )에 가 보고 싶었다.

2 아래 빈칸에 들어갈 알맞은 단어를 순서대로 쓴 것은 무엇입니까?

Which words fit in the blanks in the correct order?

- 허씨 부인은 일부러 배 좌수 앞에서 _____을/를 찼어요.
- 허씨 부인은 얼른 배 좌수의 _____을/를 살폈어요.

① 혀 – 눈치 　　② 눈치 – 혀 　　③ 발 – 표정 　　④ 표정 – 발

3 다음 중 그 뜻이 <u>다른</u> 것은 무엇입니까?

Which of the following has a <u>different</u> meaning?

① 우린 이제 인기가 더 많아질 거야.

② 우린 이제 떳떳하게 살 수 없을 거야.

③ 우린 이제 부끄러워서 살 수 없을 거야.

④ 우린 이제 얼굴을 들고 살 수 없을 거야.

4 어울리는 것끼리 연결하여 문장을 완성하세요.

Connect the matching phrases to complete the sentences.

(1) 아들을 낳아 준   •
　　허씨 부인 덕분에

• ① 더는 말 못 하고 나왔어요.

(2) 저 애들 시집보내면 •

• ② 이 집 돈이 반은 없어지겠구나.

(3) 장화가 일어나 나에게 •
　　화를 내서

• ③ 빨리 쥐도 새도 모르게
　　　　보내야지요.

(4) 날이 밝기 전에   •

• ④ 대를 이을 수 있었어요.

5 글의 내용과 <u>다른</u> 것은 무엇입니까?

Which of the following <u>is not</u> correct according to the story?

① 허씨 부인은 배 좌수에게 거짓말을 했습니다.

② 장화는 아무도 몰래 혼자서 아이를 낳았습니다.

③ 장쇠는 허씨 부인에게 쥐를 잡아 가져갔습니다.

④ 배 좌수는 결국 허씨 부인의 말을 믿게 됐습니다.

6 허씨 부인이 쥐를 죽은 아기처럼 만든 후에 어떤 일을 했습니까?
아래의 번호를 순서대로 쓰십시오.

What did Lady Heo do after making up the rat to look like a dead baby? Write the following numbers in order.

> ① 배 좌수에게 이야기했습니다.
> ② 장화와 홍련의 방으로 들어갔습니다.
> ③ 장화의 이불 속에 죽은 쥐를 넣었습니다.
> ④ 쥐를 천에 싸고 밤이 되기를 기다렸습니다.

_____ → _____ → _____ → _____

4

1 그림을 보고 알맞은 단어를 보기 에서 골라 쓰세요.

Look at the picture and choose and write out the correct words from the word bank.

| 보기 | 연못 | 숲 | 첫째 아들 | 쓰개치마 | 말 |

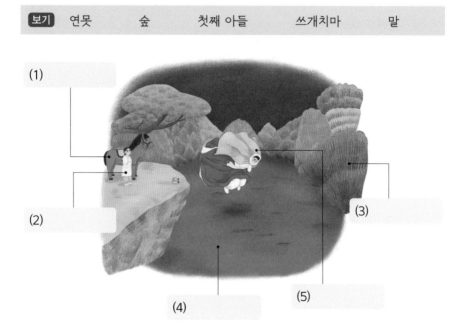

(1)

(2)

(3)

(4)

(5)

2 아래의 뜻을 보고 빈칸에 알맞은 단어를 보기 에서 골라 쓰세요.

Look at the following definitions and choose and write out the correct words from the word bank.

| 보기 | 어둡다 | 외갓집 | 산짐승 | 외할머니 | 한밤중 |

(1) (   ): 우리 어머니의 어머니

(2) (   ): 산에 사는 동물

(3) (   ): 우리 어머니의 부모님이 사는 집

(4) (   ): 아주 깊은 밤

(5) (   ): 밝지 않다는 의미

3 다음 중 틀린 것은 무엇입니까?

Which of the following is incorrect?

① 가도 가도 길이 안 나옵니다.

② 먹어도 먹어도 배가 고픕니다.

③ 들어도 들어도 다시 잊어버립니다.

④ 읽어도 읽어도 눈에 잘 들어옵니다.

4 다음은 이 글을 읽은 학생들의 반응입니다. 이 글을 잘못 이해한 학생을 고르십시오.

The following are the reactions of students who read the story. Choose the student who misunderstood the story.

① 이빙: 장화는 아직 살아 있어요.

② 준: 장화는 연못에 뛰어들었어요.

③ 다니엘: 호랑이는 진실을 알고 있어요.

④ 세자르: 장쇠는 장화를 오해하고 있네요.

5 장쇠 없이 말만 집으로 돌아왔을 때 허씨 부인의 심정으로 가장 알맞은 것을 고르세요.

Choose the answer that best matches Lady Heo's emotions when the horse returned home alone without Jangswe.

① 억울하다

② 섭섭하다

③ 걱정하다

④ 화가 나다

6 누가 한 생각입니까? 알맞게 연결하세요.

Who thought this? Connect the correct answers.

(1) '호랑이가 물어뜯다니! 하늘이 화나신 거야.' •

• ①

배 좌수

(2) '장쇠가 왜 이렇게 집에 안 돌아오지?' •

• ②

허씨 부인

5

1 그림을 보고 알맞은 단어를 보기 에서 골라 쓰세요.

Look at the picture and choose and write out the correct words from the word bank.

| 보기 | 파랑새 | 쫓아가다 | 풀밭 | 무지개 | 안개 |

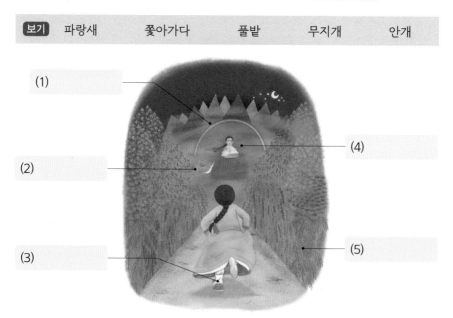

(1)

(2)

(3)

(4)

(5)

2 빈칸에 알맞은 단어를 넣어 문장을 완성하세요.

Complete the sentences by filling in the blanks with the correct words.

기억	소리	그치다	끄덕이다	눕다

(1) 파랑새가 고개를 ( )았/었어요.

(2) 그 뒤로 울음소리가 ( )지 않았어요.

(3) 그것은 너무나 ( )에 남는 꿈이었어요.

(4) 홍련이 병이 나서 자리에 ( )고 말았어요.

(5) 허씨 부인이 홍련에게 ( )을/를 질렀어요.

3 아래의 단어와 '-(으)ㄴ 적이 있다/없다'를 사용해서 과거의 경험을 뜻하는 문장을 완성하세요.

Choose the correct words from the following and use "-(으)ㄴ 적이 있다/없다" to complete the sentences to mean that something was or wasn't experienced in the past.

먹다	살다	듣다	보다	가다

(1) 이 영화를 ( )아/어요.

(2) 이 음악을 ( )아/어요.

(3) 거기에 한 번 ( )는데 경치가 아주 아름다웠어요.

(4) 한국에 여행을 가서 김치찌개를 ( )는데 너무 매웠어요.

(5) 예전에 말레이시아에서 ( )아/어서 말레이시아어를 아주 잘해요.

4 왜 홍련은 자리에 눕게 되었습니까?

Why did Hongryeon fall ill?

_____

5 글의 내용과 다른 것은 무엇입니까?

Which of the following is not correct according to the story?

① 파랑새는 장화가 어디에 있는지 알고 있었습니다.

② 홍련은 아버지에게 인사하고 연못으로 뛰어들었습니다.

③ 연못가에서 장화와 홍련의 울음소리가 매일 들렸습니다.

④ 홍련은 파랑새 덕분에 언니가 있는 곳을 알게 되었습니다.

6 누가 한 말입니까? 알맞게 연결하세요.

Who said this? Connect the correct answers.

(1) "이상한 꿈이구나. 무슨 일이
　　생긴 게 틀림없어."

　　　　　　　　　　　　　　　　　　· ①

장화

(2) "곧 너를 데리러 올게.
　　조금만 기다려."

(3) "사람은 한번 죽으면 다시
　　살아나지 못해."

　　　　　　　　　　　　　　　　　　· ②

홍련

(4) "너는 또 무슨 말로 네 아버지
　　마음을 아프게 했어?"

　　　　　　　　　　　　　　　　　　· ③

허씨 부인

<u>6</u>

1 **빈칸에 알맞은 단어를 넣어 문장을 완성하세요.**

Complete the sentences by filling in the blanks with the correct words.

반드시	내려가다	똑바로	벌을 주다	이상하다

(1) 정동우는 그날로 철산으로 ( )았/었어요.

(2) 사또는 정신을 차리고 ( ) 앉아 있었어요.

(3) 요즘 철산에서 ( )(으)ㄴ/는 일이 생기기 시작했어요.

(4) 장화와 홍련은 사또가 계모와 장쇠에게 ( )기를 바랐어요.

(5) 정동우는 자신이 ( ) 장화와 홍련의 억울함을 풀어 주고 싶었어요.

2 **아래의 단어와 '–(으)ㄹ 때'를 사용해서 어떤 행동이나 상황이 일어난 순간 혹은 지속되는 동안을 뜻하는 문장을 완성하세요.**

Choose the correct words from the following and use "–(으)ㄹ 때" to complete the sentences to mean a moment at which an action or situation happens, or a period during which it continues.

자다	돌아가다	공부하다	통화하다	계산하다

(1) 집에 ( ) 버스를 타고 가요.

(2) 밤에 ( ) 항상 라디오를 켜 놓아요.

(3) 버스 안에서 ( ) 목소리를 아주 작게 해요.

(4) 저는 외국어를 ( ) AI를 전혀 사용하지 않아요.

(5) 식당에서 음식값을 ( ) 요즘은 현금을 거의 안 써요.

3 정동우와 관련이 없는 것은 무엇입니까?

Which of the following <u>does not</u> apply to Jeong Dongwu?

① 정직하다   ② 튼튼하다

③ 답답하다   ④ 용기가 있다

4 왜 왕은 정동우를 철산으로 보냈습니까?

Why did the king send Jeong Dongwu to Cheolsan?

_____

_____

5 정동우 앞에 나타난 장화와 홍련 두 자매의 심정으로 가장 알맞은 것은 무엇입니까?

What best matches the emotions of the two sisters, Janghwa and Hongryeon, who appeared before Jeong Dongwu?

① 편하다

③ 섭섭하다

② 무섭다

④ 억울하다

6 글의 내용과 같은 것은 무엇입니까?

Which of the following is correct according to the story?

① 배 좌수는 사또에게 거짓말을 했습니다.

② 장화와 홍련은 학을 타고 사또 앞에 나타났습니다.

③ 허씨 부인은 사또에게 거짓 증거를 보여 주었습니다.

④ 두 자매는 아버지도 벌을 받아야 한다고 생각했습니다.

7

1 빈칸에 알맞은 단어를 넣어 문장을 완성하세요.

Complete the sentences by filling in the blanks with the correct words.

꺼내다	때리다	붙이다	비치다	세우다

(1) 사또가 잠시 눈을 (   )(으)려고 누웠어요.

(2) 그리고 그 무덤 위에 비석을 (   )았/었어요.

(3) 배 좌수는 울음을 그치고 이야기를 (   )았/었어요.

(4) 관청의 하인들이 허씨를 틀에 묶고 매를 (   )았/었어요.

(5) 정동우는 햇빛이 잘 (   )(으)ㄴ/는 산에 무덤을 만들었어요.

2 다음 중 사또가 한 말이 <u>아닌</u> 것은 무엇입니까?

Which of the following <u>was not</u> said by the magistrate?

① "그래, 무슨 말을 했지?"

② "이것이 죽은 아기란 말이지?"

③ "얼른 두 사람의 목에 칼을 채워라!"

④ "아니, 이건 쥐똥, 쥐똥이잖아!"

3 등장인물에 맞는 설명을 찾아 번호를 쓰세요.

Find the description that matches the character and write the number.

> ① 호랑이에게 벌을 받았습니다.
> ② 윤 씨 집안의 딸과 결혼했습니다.
> ③ 억울함을 푼 다음 인사를 하려고 왔습니다.
> ④ 거짓말을 하다가 결국 자신의 잘못을 말했습니다.
> ⑤ 두 자매의 억울한 이야기를 적어서 사람들에게 알려 주었습니다.

(1) 장화와 홍련: _____   (2) 사또: _____

(3) 배 좌수: _____   (4) 허씨 부인: _____

(5) 장쇠: _____

4 꿈에서 장화와 홍련을 본 사또에게는 어떤 일이 생겼습니까?

What happened to the magistrate who saw Janghwa and Hongryeon in a dream?

_____

5 자신이 한 일이 아닌데도 억울하게 의심받게 된다면 여러분의 심정은 어떨까요?

How would you feel if you were unfairly suspected of something that you hadn't done?

_____

_____

6 여러분이 허씨 부인의 나쁜 행동을 알았던 배 좌수라면 어떻게 행동했을까요?

What would you have done if you were Bae Jwasu and you found out about the evil thing Lady Heo had done?

_____

_____

1장

1 (1) 눈을 떴어요   (2) 태몽
(3) 기도했어요   (4) 자매
(5) 쌍둥이

2 (1) 읽으면서   (2) 열면서
(3) 들으면서   (4) 구우면서
(5) 마시면서

3 ②

4 (1) 꽃처럼 아름다운 딸
(2) 붉은 연꽃

5 (1) ②
(2) ①
(3) ②

6 ③

2장

1 (1) 거짓말   (2) 사이
(3) 마음에 걸렸어요   (4) 코끼리
(5) 키워

2 (1) 있을 수밖에 없어요
(2) 공부할 수밖에 없어요
(3) 걸을 수밖에 없어요
(4) 배울 수밖에 없어요
(5) 먹을 수밖에 없어요

3 ①

4 ②

5 집에 들어와도 마음 붙일 데가 없었기 때문입니다.

6 장화와 홍련이 아기를 괴롭힌다고 생각했기 때문입니다.

3장

1 (1) 친어머니   (2) 떠서
(3) 이해했다   (4) 떠나
(5) 무덤

2 ①

3 ①

4 (1) ④   (2) ②
(3) ①   (4) ③

5 ②

6 ④-②-③-①

4장

1 (1) 말   (2) 첫째 아들
(3) 숲   (4) 연못
(5) 쓰개치마

2 (1) 외할머니   (2) 산짐승
(3) 외갓집   (4) 한밤중
(5) 어둡다

3 ④

4 ①

5 ③

6 (1) ①
(2) ②

5장

1 (1) 무지개   (2) 파랑새
(3) 쫓아가다   (4) 안개
(5) 풀밭

2 (1) 끄덕였어요   (2) 그치
(3) 기억   (4) 눕
(5) 소리

3 (1) 본 적이 있어요/없어요
  (2) 들은 적이 있어요/없어요
  (3) 간 적이 있는데
  (4) 먹은 적이 있는데
  (5) 산 적이 있어서

4 언니가 너무 보고 싶어서 병이 났기 때문입니다.

5 ②

6 (1) ②   (2) ①
  (3) ①   (4) ③

4 더 높은 벼슬에 올라서 장군까지 되었습니다.

5 ⓔ 기분이 너무 안 좋아서 아무것도 하고 싶지
  않을 것 같습니다.

6 ⓔ 바로 관청에 신고해서 나라에서 정한 벌을
  받게 했을 것 같습니다.

6장

1 (1) 내려갔어요   (2) 똑바로
  (3) 이상한   (4) 벌을 주
  (5) 반드시

2 (1) 돌아갈 때   (2) 잘 때
  (3) 통화할 때   (4) 공부할 때
  (5) 계산할 때

3 ③

4 소문이 사실인지 알아보고 백성들의 마음을
  편하게 해 주려고 보냈습니다.

5 ④

6 ③

7장

1 (1) 붙이려고   (2) 세웠어요
  (3) 꺼냈어요   (4) 때렸어요
  (5) 비치는

2 ④

3 (1) ③   (2) ⑤
  (3) ②   (4) ④
  (5) ①

1

Two Sisters Who Lost Their Mother Early On

p.11

In the Joseon Dynasty, a person named Bae Muyong was living in Cheolsan in Pyeong-an-do Province. Although it was not a very high position among government officials, he did the work of a jwasu, so the people called him "Bae Jwasu."

Bae Jwasu had a kind and beautiful wife, Lady Jang. The couple was not lacking for money, but for a long time, had had no children. Bae Jwasu often said, "I'm already nearly 40 years old; I don't know why I don't have any children."

Lady Jang also wanted very much to have children. And she was sorry and grateful to her husband who understood her. Lady Jang prayed everyday.

"Please just send me one lovely baby."

p. 12

Then one day, Lady Jang was tired and fell asleep for a short while. In her dream, a fairy descended from the sky and gave her a flower. Lady Jang took the flower and hugged it tight to her chest. The flower turned into a beautiful fairy and went inside of Lady Jang's chest. Lady Jang awoke, eyes flying open in surprise.

Lady Jang told Bae Jwasu about her dream.

"Last night, I dreamed a very strange dream."

"What kind of dream was it?"

Bae Jwasu listened to Lady Jang's story and then spoke with great joy.

"My wife, that is a conception dream. I think the heavens know that we don't have a child

and are going to send us one."

"Could it really be? If that happened, it would be so wonderful."

And then after 10 months, Lady Jang gave birth to a truly beautiful baby. The baby's name was Janghwa. It meant "a daughter as beautiful as a flower." The couple was so happy that the baby had been born and they loved her very much.

When Janghwa turned three years old, a second baby came to the couple. This time, they hoped that a baby boy would be born.

p. 13

But it was a baby girl this time as well. The couple was a little disappointed, but they looked at their baby who had been born and felt happy. They gave their second daughter the name Hongryeon, meaning "red lotus flower."

Janghwa and Hongryeon grew well. They were three years apart, but they went everywhere together, like twins. They got along well, talking together, dancing, and playing house.

However, good things always seem to be followed by bad. Lady Jang ended up bedridden after falling ill. This was when Janghwa was seven years old and Hongryeon was four. Together with her father Bae Jwasu, the seven-year-old Janghwa didn't leave Lady Jang's side and helped her to take her medicine every day. They tried every medication that was said to be good, but Lady Jang didn't recover.

"My wife, think of our young daughters and recover, please."

"I'm sorry, darling. I might have to leave our poor children and close my eyes for the last time..."

p.14

"Mother. Don't say things like that. Take your medicine now and grow healthy and get better. All right?"
However, the lady Jang's body got weaker and weaker and she lost more and more weight. She couldn't even breathe well. Lady Jang was barely breathing when she spoke to Bae Jwasu.
"Darling, when I die... Please take good care of our two daughters, Janghwa and Hongryeon. Raise those poor... children well, marry a good person, and live happily for a long, long time... please. If... you'll grant my wish, then even after I die... I won't forget my gratitude to you."
"Why are you talking like that? Stop worrying and recover, quickly now."
"I worry that after I die... a new wife will come and our children won't be able to receive their father's love. P- promise me, p-... please. Take care... of Janghwa and Hong...ryeon..."
When Lady Jang raised her hand with difficulty, Bae Jwasu grabbed it and spoke.
"I promise. Don't worry about that and get better."
Lady Jang, who had exhausted all her strength and finished speaking, closed her eyes.
"My wife! My wife!"
"Mother! Mother!"

p. 15

Bae Jwasu began to cry, and Janghwa held the young Hongryeon and cried loudly as well. They buried Lady Jang in the mountains, and Janghwa and Hongryeon were so sad that they couldn't sleep and did nothing but cry.
Time passed and the three years of mourning

for Lady Jang ended, but the sadness of the sisters Janghwa and Hongryeon, who had lost their mother, only grew deeper.

2
The Mean Stepmother, Lady Heo

p. 16

Three years passed after the death of Lady Jang. No sounds of laughter or singing came from the house any longer. Janghwa and Hongryeon were raised lonely and quietly. The sight of his sad daughters made their father's heart ache. The words of his late wife troubled Bae Jwasu's mind, but he had no son to carry on his family name and he worried terribly. He also no longer wished to see his daughters without a mother, so he decided to marry again.

p.17

Bae Jwasu asked this person and that, and looked for someone who would become Janghwa and Hongryeon's stepmother.
"I hope I can find someone strong who will take good care of my daughters and help

carry on my family name."
He was introduced to people from all over, but they all looked weak and he didn't like them. Among them, the one who looked strongest was a woman who had the surname Heo. Bae Jwasu, seeing Lady Heo for the first time, was shocked. There was a rash across her face and her two eyes were too large, her mouth stuck out too much, her waist was thick, and her legs were like those of an elephant. Her appearance was so ugly that it was difficult to look at her for too long, and her personality was even worse.
However, thinking that it was fine so long as her body was strong, Bae Jwasu married Lady Heo. But oh, dear! As Lady Heo didn't like the young Janghwa and Hongryeon from the very first day she came to her husband's house, the atmosphere inside the house changed greatly. Every day, the house was noisy and loud sound was constantly made.
"What's this? Why are you giving leftover food to the neighbors? Go and get it back."
"Hurry up and go cut some grass to make more manure!"

"Get up quickly and get to work, and bring back firewood."

p. 18

Lady Heo constantly ordered the servants to work. And she didn't simply leave Janghwa and Hongryeon alone as well. She ordered her daughters to work without rest.
"You two sew these clothes again by tomorrow!"
"Are you playing in your room again? If you have nothing to do, go take these peppers and lay them out one by one in the sun."

p. 20

Bae Jwasu was shocked to see this. He felt nothing but apologetic toward Janghwa and Hongryeon, who were having a difficult time because of their wicked stepmother.

'She's really a bad person. I married in a rush, but things in the future will be an even bigger problem. And if I tell her this and that about how to raise the children, I'll lose face.'

Bae Jwasu, who hadn't the heart for it, started not to come home very often. When he sometimes came home early, he always heard the sound of Janghwa and Hongryeon crying. Bae Jwasu was so frustrated that he spoke to Lady Heo.

"Come now, nobody has died, so why is it that I hear the sounds of this crying every day?"

"Come now, yeonggam. Why are you asking me that? No matter what I say, they cry sadly like that. It seems they certainly cry like a river. And *yeonggam*, when was it exactly that they didn't cry? They were always crying even before I came here."

p. 21

Bae Jwasu could not respond to that. Because what Lady Heo said was not wrong. It was true that after their mother had died, Janghwa and Hongryeon had cried a lot. And so even when he saw his daughters crying, there was nothing Bae Jwasu could do but keep quiet. And of course, the servants avoided Lady Heo.

Time passed and the two of them had a child. The child Lady Heo gave birth to was a son. After this, she smoothly gave birth to three more sons in a row. Bae Jwasu was happy about the birth of the son that he had waited for.

One day, when Lady Heo was away, Janghwa and Hongryeon went into the main room. They wanted to hold their little baby brother once.

"Oh, how cute."

Hongryeon held the baby carefully, but he

suddenly started to cry.

"Huh? Why is the baby crying? Sister, what should I do?"

"I think he's uncomfortable that you're holding him. Put him down here again."

Just then, the door opened and Lady Heo came in angrily.

"What on earth are you two doing?"

p. 22

"Oh, Mother. The baby is so lovely that we wanted to hold him just once, but he suddenly..."

"My, my, you certainly lie well. You must have picked on him. He suddenly cried?"

"It's true, Mother. My sister and I really wanted to hold him just once."

"Lies!"

Lady Heo yelled angrily at Janghwa but Hongryeon. No matter how they tried to explain, she didn't believe them.

"Liars! Where do you think this is for you to come in here?"

Janghwa was unable to say anything but cried, and Hongryeon said, "Mother, we're sorry," through tears.

"You terrible little things! Every day you cry and tell lies! That's why your mother died early."

Lady Heo continued, saying awful things to Janghwa and Hongryeon as if it were nothing at all. Then, when her strength was entirely drained, she told Janghwa and Hongryeon to get out. Janghwa and Hongryeon came out of the main room and went into theirs. In the dark room, the sisters thought, "Where has Father gone? Why did we get scolded?" They grew sadder and sadder, and the children began to cry again.

"Mom. M-mom. M-m-mom!"

3

Stepmother's Wicked Lie

p. 23

Bae Jwasu was well aware that Lady Heo had a terrible personality. However, because of Lady Heo, who had borne him three sons, he was able to carry on his family name. So even though there were things he didn't like, he simply passed them by.

Janghwa and Hongryeon grew old enough to marry. Each time he saw them, Bae Jwasu's heart hurt and he pitied them. He was so very sorry to his wife Lady Jang, who had passed before him. So he would sometimes go into the two children's room and talk to his daughters about their mother.

"Father, I'd like to go to Mother's grave once."

"All right, if you want to see your mother, you should go. I want to see her too."

"No, I'll just hold it in. I'll meet Mother in my dreams, like Hongryeon."

"But why? Because you're scared of your stepmother?"

Bae Jwasu knew that it was because of Lady Heo.

p. 24

"Janghwa, I know you're saying that because of your stepmother. Just hang in there for a little while. I'll get a matchmaker and hurry up and find you a good husband."

Those words were a promise to prepare a lot of money for a wedding and marry the girls into good families. Janghwa and Hongryeon understood everything their father said.

But Lady Heo was listening to these words from outside.

'This is a big problem. If those girls are married off, half of the family's money will be gone. Then what will become of my sons? I'll be the dog that chased the chickens onto the roof, stuck doing nothing but twiddling my fingers, won't I?'

When she thought about it, this was no small problem. The family's many belongings and money had originally been brought by Lady Jang, Janghwa and Hongryeon's real mother. So even if the two daughters took everything, she wouldn't be able to say anything about it. From that day on, Lady Heo didn't eat. She couldn't sleep and her head hurt. She laid in her room for several days and thought and thought.

'What do I do? What should I do? Is there no good method I can use?'

p. 25

At last, Lady Heo thought of one very terrible method indeed.

'Hehehe, that's right, doing it like that'll be good. Wait! First I'll have to catch a rat.'

A few days later, Lady Heo called for her first son, Jangswe, and spoke.

"Jangswe, you know how to catch a rat, right?"

"Hey, of course I know how. I can catch a rat as big as my forearm with nothing but my hands."

"Then you go catch a big one and bring it here to your mother."

Jangswe went to the storeroom and set a rattrap, and before evening, he had caught a rat the size of his forearm and brought it to his mother.

Lady Heo went to the bathroom and, without anybody knowing, made the rat up to look like a dead baby.

Then she wrapped the rat in cloth and waited

for night to fall. When it was night, Lady Heo went into Janghwa and Hongryeon's room. The two sisters were sleeping deeply.

'I have to do this before Jwasu yeonggam comes. Better hurry.'

Lady Heo placed the dead rat inside of Janghwa's bedsheets. And then she quickly left the room.

Bae Jwasu finished work and came home. Lady Heo deliberately clicked her tongue in front of him. He thought it was strange, so he asked.

p. 26

"My wife, your face is odd today. Did something happen?"

"W-well, I, I'm so shocked that I can't say it."

Lady Heo didn't tell him right away.

"What is it that you can't say? Go on and tell me."

"Oh, mercy, I didn't raise our daughters well. My goodness, sob, sob! It's obvious yeonggam won't believe me... What am I to do now?"

"Now now, what is it that's got you like this? Is it something to do with Janghwa and Hongryeon?"

Lady Heo quickly read Bae Jwasu's face. He looked as if he would listen to everything Lady Heo had to say, no matter what it was. So she began to say the words she had prepared.

"The girls didn't come out of their room all day today so I thought they might be sick and went to look. Well, there was blood on the floor of their room and I saw a small lump of flesh coming out of the blankets, so I asked what it was. Janghwa woke up and got mad at me, so I couldn't say any more and left."

"What are you saying?"

"Yeonggam, I think that without a doubt, she played with a man and something happened."

"What kind of nonsense are you saying right now? That can't be! My daughter Janghwa would never!"

p. 27

"Hmph! The day you believe me is the day the sun rises in the west. That's why from the start I said that you wouldn't believe me, didn't I? I wonder what you'll say when you go into the room right now and have a look."

Bae Jwasu was simply sitting there with an unbelieving expression on his face. But he couldn't stay like that. He carefully went into Janghwa's room. Like Lady Heo had said, there was blood on the floor of the room. Looking in between the sheets, there was a red lump of flesh. Bae Jwasu couldn't even think to wake Janghwa and ask her what had happened, and quickly opened the door and ran out.

"What am I to do? Oh!"

Lady Heo spoke then, as if she had been waiting.

"Yeonggam, if the neighbors find out about this, no good will come of it. Try telling them that a young woman gave birth to a child and killed it, all before she even got married. We won't be able to live showing our faces anymore, with that loss of face in a gentleman's house."

"Then what should we do about this? Please, tell me, my wife."

Even as she was pleased on the inside, Lady Heo spoke with a worried expression.

p. 28

"All we can do is let Janghwa leave here and go to a distant place where she won't be seen."

"Far away? Where do you mean?"

"A place that's out of sight. Before day breaks, we have to send her quickly without anyone knowing."

"Where is there such a place?"

"Her grave!"

"H-her grave?"

"Yes, yeonggam. With me saying this, you'll tell me that I'm a stepmother trying to kill your former wife's child, but there's no other way. If we don't do it, then we'll all have to die. As a *yangban*(gentleman), you'll lose face and everything else. Isn't that the same as losing one's life?"

"Th, that's true, but still, how could I take my living child and.... Isn't there any better idea?"

"I've thought it over. But if she lives, she'll have to live in shame until she dies, and if people find out about it, the other children won't be able to marry either! So you need to decide quickly, yeonggam."

The more he thought about it, the more it seemed Lady Heo was right. He had no other choice, and the Bae Jwasu decided to do as his wife had said.

4
Janghwa Faces an Unjust Death

p. 29

Lady Heo called for Jangswe to prepare horse, and spoke something to him quietly. Then she went to wake Janghwa.

Janghwa heard a strange sound and opened her eyes in surprise. It was the sound of her being called to from outside.

"Janghwa, wake up."

"Yes? Oh, yes, Mother!"

Janghwa, who had heard Lady Heo calling, got up and went outside.

"Your maternal grandmother is calling for you in a hurry. She says she wants to see you in place of your mother. You'll have to go now and follow Jangswe to your grandparents' house."

"R-right now?"

"Yes, you have to go quickly. Jangswe will take you."

To Janghwa's mind, it seemed as if something bad had happened. So she said she would change her clothes and go, and went back into her room and woke up Hongryeon.

p. 30

"Hongryeon, your big sister has to go to our maternal grandparents' house."

"To our grandparents house? Why?"

"I don't know either. She says I have to go quickly... But I'm still anxious to leave you alone. Let's change into each other's clothes. Then if you miss your big sister, you can look at these clothes and think of me. Got it?"

"Sister, don't go! Tell Father you aren't going. Okay?"

"I can't. It'll be all right. Grandmother's calling for me so I'll go quickly and come back. Stay well, Hongryeon."

She rushed to dress and went back outside. She saw the figure of her father standing in the dark. As Janghwa bowed her head in farewell, Jangswe appeared with a horse.

"Quickly, get on. I can't sleep because of you, Elder Sister. What is all this?"

Jangswe got Janghwa to ride the horse and went outside.

They went on and on, but the road didn't appear and they kept heading deep into the mountains. It was frightening as they kept on hearing the cries of wild animals.

"Jangswe, I'm scared. Are you sure this is the way to my grandparents' house?"

"Come on, do you think you're the only one who's scared? I'm scared too. So let's go quietly."

p. 31

Jangswe said this and then went even deeper into the woods. The sound of running water in the dark forest sounded like the cries of a ghost.

At last, a pond appeared deep in the mountains. It looked very deep. But Jangswe suddenly stopped the horse near the pond.

"Elder Sister, you can get off here."

"N-no, J-Jangswe. Get off here by this dark pond?"

"If you get off, I'll tell you why."

Jangswe waited until Janghwa got off of the horse.

"Elder Sister, you did a very shameful thing that you shouldn't have done. Mother told me. She said that you'd have to pay for your crime with your life. I came here to show you the way. The talk of going to your grandparents' house was a lie."

"W-what? When did I? Where? What was it, and how did I do it?"

"Come on, Elder Sister. Why are you getting angry at me? Aren't you ashamed that you gave birth to a child before even getting married?"

"How can you say that!"

"Mother and Father know all about it."

p. 32

"Jangswe, I didn't. I didn't do it. I didn't do such a ridiculous thing!"

"Now now, stop talking and hurry up. Lay down your life, since you've made it impossible for the rest of the family to live showing their faces."

Without even batting an eye, Jangswe told her to jump in the pond and drown.

Only then did Janghwa understand that her stepmother meant to kill her, and she sat on the ground and began to cry.

"Oh, heavens above! How can only such terrible things happen to me? If I die like this, who will know my feelings of injustice? Who will protect my poor Hongryeon?"

Janghwa's words rang out through the deep mountains. But Jangswe was still simply standing there yawning, as if he couldn't be bothered.

"We came all the way here, so let's do it quickly. Otherwise, we might get bitten to death by a wild animal. And I want to go home quickly and go to sleep. What's all this commotion in the middle of the night for? I'm dying of exahustion."

Janghwa begged her younger brother for help.

She said she would go far away and never appear again, and asked him to save her. But Jangswe told her to hurry up and got angry.

p. 33

So scared that her body trembled, Janghwa took off her shoes. With tears in her eyes, she made one last request of Jangswe.

"Jangswe, I'm dying unfairly because of something I haven't done, but please take care of poor Hongryeon. Oh, poor Hongryeon! I'm sorry to leave you and go first."

And then Janghwa put her covering skirt over her head and jumped into the pond with a splash.

p. 34

Just at that moment, a large tiger appeared with a "roar!"
"Oh! A t-t-tiger!"
Jangswe was so scared that even though he wanted to run, his feet were frozen to the spot and wouldn't move.
"Roar! You're a wicked one. That mother and her son! You louse! Killing your poor, kind sister! I won't let you get away! Roar!"
And then the tiger bit off one of Jangswe's ears, one of his arms, and one of legs. Jangswe blacked out just like that, blood flowing. The startled horse ran straight back home.
No matter how long Lady Heo waited, Jangswe didn't come back. When only the horse came back, it seemed like something had happened. She sent the servants to find Jangswe. They found Jangswe, who had lost an arm and a leg, near the pond, and brought him back. Lady Heo quickly treated his

wounds and prepared medicine, which she gave to him. Bae Jwasu looked at the injured Jangswe, who had been bitten by a tiger, and was frightened. He thought that something had gone wrong.
'Bitten by a tiger! The heavens are angered. Then what has become of Janghwa?'

5

Hongryeon Jumps Into the Pond to Follow Her Sister

p. 35

"Sister! Sister! Where are you going all by yourself?" Hongryeon said, crying. Janghwa looked back at her and spoke through tears.
"Hongryeon, I'm sorry. You and I have different paths. I'm very busy right now so I can't speak for long. But I'll come for you soon. Just wait a little while."
Janghwa finished speaking and Hongryeon awoke, startled. It had been a dream. A dream she remembered very well!
'What a strange dream. No doubt something has happened to my sister.'
Hongryeon gathered her courage and asked her father.
"Father, I saw my sister in a dream again today. My sister, who said she would go to our grandparents' house and come back, isn't coming and she keeps appearing in my dreams just crying. I'm sure that something has happened."
Bae Jwasu listened to Hongryeon's words and felt as if he were short of breath. And then he just cried without saying a word.

p. 36

"Yeonggam, what's the matter? Hongryeon, what have you done now to upset your father? Can't you get out of here? Quickly." Lady Heo ran in suddenly and shouted at Hongryeon. At her stepmother's words, Hongryeon left her father's room. Hongryeon missed her sister so much that she got sick. And just like that, she ended up falling ill. But Lady Heo made life even harder for Hongryeon, who had been left alone.

One day, when Lady Heo had gone out, Hongryeon, who hadn't eaten anything for several days, barely managed to get up. Then she called for Jangswe and asked him again and again what had happened to Janghwa. Jangswe finally told her about Janghwa. After listening to the whole story, Hongryeon sank to the floor.

'So that's it! That's why she cried so sadly. Stepmother lied to Father and had my sister killed!'

Hongryeon cried sadly. Tears sprang to her eyes at just the site of the yard out back where she'd played with her sister, and the blanket and hairbrush they'd shared.

'Sister, this is too much. How could you leave me alone and go? Take me with you...'

p. 37

Hongryeon, who didn't want to live any longer, thought that she ought to follow her older sister. But she had never gone anywhere outside of the house before and could not find the pond where her sister had died. And then, one night, when Hongryeon was sitting with the door to her room open, a blue bird flew into the flower garden. It moved from this flower to that, and didn't leave the garden. It was so strange that

Hongryeon went outside and chased after the blue bird.

'Could this be my older sister, who turned into a blue bird and came here?'

Hongryeon, who had that thought, asked a favor of the blue bird.

"Blue bird, do you know where my older sister is? If you know, tell me, too."

And then, as if it understood what Hongryeon said, the blue bird nodded its head, did it not? Then it flew off ahead a little bit. Hongryeon quietly opened the front gate so that it wouldn't make a sound and went outside of the house.

The blue bird turned in circles and flew off ahead. And then it came back, and flew ahead again, and came back again. It showed Hongryeon the way. Hongryeon followed the blue bird out of the village. She passed through a meadow and went into the forest.

p. 38

The sun set and it became night. Hongryeon arrived at a pond with a moonbow floating above it. But then suddenly, the blue bird circled the pond and cried out sadly.

'Oh, it's here. My sister is here. I should go in there too.'

Weeping, Hongryeon looked at the pond. But just then, she heard a sad woman's voice coming from inside of the fog.

"Hongryeon! Hongryeoooooon!"

"S-sister? Sister? Janghwa!" Hongryeon shouted joyfully.

"That's right, Hongryeon. Welcome. I sent a blue bird to you because I have something I must tell you. Listen to me carefully. Once a person dies, they can't come back to life again. Life is precious. So go back home,

quickly. Please, I beg you, Hongryeon."
"No, Sister. I can't live in a world without you anymore. I want to go with you too. When you died unjustly, I didn't want to live anymore either. Oh, God! I'm going to follow my sister too. Please, just relieve my sister of her injustice."

p. 40

Hongryeon, who cried as she spoke, jumped up, bowed deeply to the heavens, covered her head with her clothing, and jumped into the water.
"Hongryeon! Hongryeoooooon!"
"Sob! Sisteeeeer!"
Afterwards, the sounds of crying didn't stop. Day and night, crying could be heard near the pond. Anyone who came into the forest or passed by on the path could hear it.

6

The Magistrate Who Relieves the Sisters of Their Resentment

p. 41

But strange things began to happen. In Cheolsan, the harvest went poorly, and more and more people died because they couldn't eat. Bit by bit, the number of people in the village decreased, so the country sent a new magistrate. But each new magistrate that arrived died without even staying one night, and this continued to happen.
The king learned about this and was also very worried.
"This sort of thing is happening in Cheolsan, so who would go down there to help the people?"
Not one of his vassals wanted to go. They recommended Jeong Dongwu, who was strong and honest, and very courageous as well. The king was very pleased to see Jeong Dongwu.
"The people are having great difficulties because of what's happening in Cheolsan. Go there quickly and find out if the rumors are true, and put the people's minds at ease."

p. 42

Jeong Dongwu went down to Cheolsan that day. When he arrived at the village, he called for the *yibang* and asked in detail about what had happened up until now.
"Yibang! Is it true that each of the magistrates who came here died without even spending one night?"
"Yes, that's right. It's a bit strange to tell you this, but they all died in just one day. But

even until now, we don't know the reason why."

The magistrate closed his eyes and thought. And then he called for some men from the government office and spoke.

"You all, don't sleep tonight. Stay alert and watch carefully to see what happens."

The magistrate turned the lights on bright and began to read a book. Deep in the night, he began to grow sleepy. But suddenly, a cold wind blew and the lights went out. The magistrate came alert and sat up straight. Just then, a woman suddenly appeared and quietly bowed.

p. 43

"Who-who are you? Are you a ghost? Are you a person?"

The magistrate spoke out loud. And then the woman, who was wearing a white hanbok, stood up and bowed once more.

"Magistrate, I'm sorry to suddenly come find you late at night. I'm Hongryeon, the daughter of Bae Muyong, the jwasu of this village. But I died because of something so unjust that I came to find you like this."

The ghost was Hongryeon, who had followed her older sister and ended her own life. Hongryeon spoke in detail about the things that had happened within her family. The magistrate wasn't frightened, and sat still and listened to all of Hongryeon's story. When Hongryeon finished speaking, she stood up and bowed, and then left.

The startled magistrate couldn't sleep until morning.

'Isn't it because of this matter that the village of Cheolsan has become like this?'

Early the next morning, the magistrate went to the government office. At the appearance of the magistrate, who had spent the night and not died, everyone was shocked. The magistrate asked the yibang if there was a jwasu called Bae Muyong in the village.

"Yes, there is. I heard that he's living well through the inheritance of his late wife."

"Then that means he has a new wife. How many children does he have?"

"The two daughters he had with his late wife died, and he has three sons from his new wife."

p. 44

"How did his two daughters die?"

"According to rumor, they say that the older daughter committed a sin and drowned in a lake, and the younger sister, who learned of her older sister's death, cried sadly and followed her, and died too. Since then, when someone passes by the lake, they can hear the sad sound of the two girls crying, so people are frightened when they pass by there."

Having heard what the yibang said, the magistrate called right away for Bae Jwasu and Lady Heo. The magistrate asked the two of them, who were caught and brought to him by the men at the government office, about Janghwa and Hongryeon. Bae Jwasu trembled as he answered.

"How can I lie when you ask me even though you already know?"

Because even Hongryeon had left home, Bae Jwasu had been unable to speak to anyone and had been frustrated all by himself. He slowly began to tell the story of how Janghwa had given birth to a child.

"Then bring me proof that she gave birth to a child."

Lady Heo took out a small cloth and showed

it to the magistrate as she spoke.
"Goodness, Magistrate. If you mean this, I brought it with me. I was so surprised that I couldn't throw it away and kept it like this."

p. 45

The magistrate looked at the item and his head spun.
"Then I'll call for you again after I look into this a little more. You can leave for today."
Looking at Lady Heo, who kept speaking loudly as she left, the magistrate grew angry.
'Even if she's the stepmother, she goes too far. So, despite being yangban class, she doesn't even think about saving face and speaks too easily about her daughter's wrongdoing! But then what is the unjust thing the woman from last night meant? There's even proof of the misdeed... But it's strange...'
Then, when night fell, a cold wind blew and the woman from last night came to find him again. This time, Janghwa and Hongryeon

appeared together and bowed to the magistrate. And then Hongryeon begged him, crying.
"Magistrate, our stepmother is lying. When you see that dead baby again tomorrow, open its stomach. Then relieve us of our injustice and punish stepmother and Jangswe. But please forgive our father. He met the wrong wife and was fooled by her lies."

p. 46

Then the door opened and blue cranes appeared. The two sisters, who had finished speaking, got onto the cranes and flew away.
"I absolutely must relieve those two people of their injustice."

7

The Wicked Meet Their End

p. 48

The next morning arrived. The magistrate called again for Bae Jwasu and Lady Heo. And he told them to bring out the dead baby once more.

"This is the dead baby, correct?"

"Yes, that's right, Magistrate."

"You know what will happen to you if this is a lie, right?"

The magistrate told them to open up the stomach of the dead baby where Lady Heo could see it, and then he spoke.

"Now, everyone look closely. What is this?"

Lady Heo was so surprised that she fell backwards. Bae Jwasu was shaking as he began to cry. The men from the government office who were standing to the side also looked and shouted in surprise.

"Wait, those are rat droppings, rat droppings, aren't they? Is there anyone so wicked in the whole world?"

"Quickly, put a pillory around the necks of these two! And you two, tell me the whole truth in detail!"

p. 49

Bae Jwasu was very sad and began to cry. After a short while, he stopped crying and began to tell his story.

"Lady Jang, the mother of Janghwa and Hongryeon, was a very kind and wonderful person. But she passed away without any sons and left behind two daughters. After carrying out three years of mourning, I sought out a strong new wife to carry on my family name. Her personality seemed bad, but I

hoped she would get along well with my two daughters. But one day, she told me..."

"Right, what did she tell you?"

"Yes, Magistrate. My wife told me this. She said that as a stepmother, it was difficult to tell me, but Janghwa had gotten into big trouble. At first, I didn't believe it, but there was blood on my daughter's sheets and it really looked like she had given birth to a child. And that's how it went......."

This time, the magistrate asked Lady Heo. But until the very last, Lady Heo said that she had done nothing wrong. The servants from the government office tied her to a frame and lashed her. At last, Lady Heo told the truth.

"Magistrate, it's my fault that Janghwa died. It's because I thought that when she got married, she'd take all of the family's money and many posessions, and then I wouldn't be able to give anything to my sons. I committed a crime that can't be forgiven. But my son Jangswe was already punished by a tiger, so please, just save my son."

p. 50

Still, as Jangswe's mother, lady Heo begged him to just to spare her child.

"Then what happened to the younger sister, Hongryeon?"

"After Ho-Hongryeon d-disappeared
somewhere, we s-... still haven't heard any
news about her."
"You're a very wicked person indeed.
Hongryeon followed her older sister and died.
As you very well know!"

p. 51

Lady Heo was so scared that she couldn't
speak a word. Of course, the magistrate put
not only Lady Heo in a pillory but her son
Jangswe as well. And then he told the king.
The magistrate killed the wicked Lady Heo
and Jangswe, and spared the life of Bae
Jwasu.
A few days later, the magistrate and the men
from the government office went together
to the pond where Janghwa and Hongryeon
had died. The sound of the wind sounded
like the crying of the two sisters. Over the
course of a few days, they had the servants
draw all of the water from the lake. At last, in
the deepest part of the lake, they found the
two dead sisters. Even though they had been
in the water for a long time, they looked just
as they had when they were alive. Everyone
was surprised.
"Look at that! How can they be so clean?"
The magistrate changed the two sisters'
clothes. After he laid them in a coffin, he
wrote down their unjust story and to tell it to
the people.
And then he built their grave on a mountain
that received plenty of sunlight and put up a
tombstone.
The magistrate lay down and closed his eyes
to rest for a short while, but Janghwa and
Hongryeon suddenly appeared and bowed
deeply to him.

p. 52

"Magistrate, thank you for relieving us of our
injustice and taking us out of the water. And
thank you so much for forgiving our father's
sins. Magistrate, you will soon rise to a high
government position. We sisters will take our
leave now, Magistrate. Stay well."
When the magistrate opened his eyes,
everything was as it had been.
"Oh! The sisters who were relieved of their
resentment came to express their gratitude!"
After that, the magistrate rose to a higher
position in the government and later became
a general.
Janghwa and Hongryeon's father, Bae Jwasu,
was left alone and lived missing his two
daughters. The villagers, who felt sorry for
poor Bae Jwasu, introduced him to the
daughter of the Yoon family. The two of them
married and had twin daughters who looked
exactly like Janghwa and Hongryeon.
So once more, they gave them the names
Janghwa and Hongryeon. They raised the
twin daughters with love and married them to
twin brothers who won first place in the civil
service examination. And they all lived very
pleasantly and happily.

MEMO

MEMO

Darakwon Korean Readers

장화홍련전
The Story of Janghwa and Hongryeon

Adapted by Kim Yu Mi, Yoon Kyeong Won
Translated by Jamie Lypka
First Published May, 2024
First Printing May, 2024
Publisher Chung Kyudo
Editor Lee Suk-hee, Sohn YeoRam, Baek Da-heuin
Cover Design Yoon Ji-young
Interior Design Yoon Ji-young, Yoon Hyun-ju
Illustrator SOUDAA
Voice Actor Shin So-yun, Kim Rae-whan

Published by Darakwon, Inc.
Darakwon Bldg., 211 Munbal-ro, Paju-si, Gyeonggi-do
Republic of Korea 10881
Tel : 02-736-2031 Fax : 02-732-2037
(Marketing Dept. ext.: 250~252, Editorial Dept. ext.: 420~426)

ISBN 978-89-277-3335-5 14710
      978-89-277-3259-4 (set)

Visit the Darakwon homepage to learn about our other
publications and promotions and to download the contents of
the MP3 format.

http://www.darakwon.co.kr
http://koreanbooks.darakwon.co.kr